CK f2 50p

D1267959

epublic of China

CHINA

OLD AND NEW

CHINA

OLD AND NEW

BY

JOHN LOGAN

Printed by Yee Tin Tong Printing Press Ltd.,
Tong Chong Street, Quarry Bay, Hongkong.

Contents

Illustrations

Foreword

Some 10 years after the end of the World War I conditions in the interior of China became so bad that it became dangerous for foreign business men to live there, particularly if they had no knowledge of the language. My employers, the British American Tobacco Co. Ltd., which had a large sales organisation and stocks of its cigarettes all over the country, met this situation by sending out six young men from their headquarters in London to learn the language and be responsible for the interests of the company and its Chinese employees in the interior. I was one of them and had a contract to serve for four years in China, of which one and a half years were spent learning the language and two and a half years travelling as an inspector all over the provinces of Hebei, Henan, Shanxi, and Shaanxi, all in North China: I must have covered fully 15,000 miles during this period. It was an experience which brought me in close touch with the Chinese people at many levels; I liked what I saw of them and determined to return after I had retired.

I have been back three times—in 1974, 1977 and 1980—on the first occasion by myself, on the second with my son on the Trans Siberian Railway and on the third with a large international group of tour operators and travel agents. Nothing has changed my mind about the sterling qualities of the Chinese people—their cheerfulness in adversity, their patience and stoicism, their good manners, their industry, their thought for old people and their love of peace.

This is the first book I have written and I would not have persevered with it but for the constant encouragement of Sir Robert Scott GCMG, CBE. whom I first knew as a language student for the consular service in Peking and who subsequently became British Commissioner for Southeast Asia and then the first civilian ever to have been the Commandant of the Imperial Defence College. The other person who gave me great help was the Hon. Terence Prittie, MBE, Guardian correspondent in Germany for 24 years, author of many books and an escaper with me from a German prison camp in 1941 while Dr. John Chinnery, lecturer in Chinese at Edinburgh University, kindly read and corrected the script.

J. L

I
Peking, 1928—1930

IT WAS difficult to find a job in the late 1920s, just before the great depression in the 1930s. I was 21, spoke fluent German, had some rudimentary knowledge of accountancy, was foot-loose and fancy free, and looking for some adventure in the wide open spaces of the world. Luck was on my side, when, through a personal recommendation, I was taken on, early in 1928, as a trainee in that great, world-wide organisation, the British American Tobacco Co. Ltd., at the princely starting salary of 45 shillings, or 2 pounds 25 pence a week.

The company's head office was in Millbank, Westminster, where there were quite a number of trainees. All of us knew we would be sent abroad, but no-one knew to what country; nor was anyone asked if he had a preference for any particular part of the world. It was no surprise, therefore, when six of us were summoned one afternoon to the office of a director, who was an American. The door closed and, without further ado, he said, "You are all going to China. Any objections?" None were forthcoming and, after a slight pause, we were each handed, for immediate signature, a four year contract of service in China, at the end of which period we would be granted three months home leave. I piped up, and said I would like to read the contract before signing it, which undoubtedly created an undesirable precedent. However, permission was granted: my five companions signed there and then, and I was told to bring my contract back the next day. I was sure I had made an inauspicious start to my new career by this effrontery. The elaborate consultative and interviewing procedures developed by modern personnel departments, the sort of "How do you feel about going to China?" approach, didn't exist at this time. You simply got your marching orders, and went.

From then on the six of us foregathered every day to discuss this tremendous turn of events, and to pool any knowledge we might have about China, which was precious little, except that the father of one of our number was serving in the China Consular Service. We were given some factory experience in a London cigarette factory, and a short course in Chinese Mandarin at the School of Oriental Studies (now part of the School of Oriental and African Studies). Details of the journey to China

SS *Karmala*

then arrived; we were to sail from Tilbury in the 7000 ton P. & O. steamer *Karmala* on September 14th, which was expected to reach Shanghai on October 26th, having called at Port Said, Port Sudan, Colombo, Penang, Singapore, Port Swettenham and Hong Kong, the long life line of the British Empire, protected by the Royal Navy.

She was a single funnel passenger/cargo ship with a small passenger list, the slow passage of which made the voyage such an unforgettable experience—the "gully gully" divers at Port Said, who retrieved coins and other articles from incredible depths—the slow rhythmic chanting of the coal-black dockers at Port Sudan, as they loaded and unloaded ships' cargoes—the teeth of the people at Colombo, red from chewing betel nut—the newly arrived graving dock at Singapore, so soon to fall into the hands of the Japanese—the sweaty jungle at Port Swettenham— the junks and sampans alongside ocean-going steamers, and the hustle, bustle and chatter at Hongkong, and finally the slow passage up the muddy waters of the Huangpu River to Shanghai. We were six weeks under way in our slow moving ship: today it takes some 17 hours flying time from London, with one stop in Dubai, India or Pakistan. The air journey differs little from any other one, unless one is lucky enough to fly over the Himalayas in daylight. How much the "jetter" misses in the feverish haste to reach destinations at maximum speed!

Shanghai was one of the first five treaty ports opened to foreign

4

trade by the Treaty of Nanking in 1842, which followed the Opium War. Until the arrival of foreigners, it had been a medium-sized walled town on the Huangpu River, a minor tributary of the great Yangtse River. The British concession, created in 1843, subsequently became an international settlement in 1863, the French having acquired a separate concession in 1847. Later, after the disastrous defeat of the Chinese in the Sino-Japanese War, the Japanese concession in the north of the city was created by the Treaty of Shimonoseki in 1895.

Shanghai, ideally situated for trade up the Yangtse, the world's third longest river, became the most important of all the treaty ports, and handled well over 50 per cent of all foreign trade, until the advent of the Japanese in 1937, and the subsequent blockade of the river: it is by far the biggest industrial centre in Communist China today, and, with a population of well over 10 million, one of the biggest cities in the world. Old China hands, who read this book, may be astonished to know that, in 1977, there were exactly seven holders of British passports in this great city, of which four were university students and three connected with the Hongkong and Shanghai, and Chartered Banks respectively. The two bank employees, one of them married, were finding life pretty uncongenial—neither of them spoke Chinese; their assignment to Shanghai was for 15 months.

Dominating the scene in front of the riverside Bund, where most of the stately prestigious buildings of the biggest foreign firms were situated, lay the 10,000-ton British cruiser *Cumberland*. Smaller warships and gunboats of other nationalities were to be seen, with sampans and junks in profusion. Further down river, large ocean-going steamers were loading and unloading, a scene of constant movement and activity. The vast majority of those living in the international settlement were Chinese, many of whom regarded it as a safe haven for their fortunes, and a refuge from the constant civil wars in the interior.

In due course the five of us (one of our number had been dropped off in Hongkong) visited the firm's headquarters, where we were told that we were going to a language school in Peking for 18 months, to learn Mandarin. Most of the foreign employees, few of whom spoke Chinese, had been withdrawn from the interior owing to the banditry and constant civil wars. We, with our newly won command of the language, were to replace them as travelling inspectors of the various, widely-scattered sub-offices, all of which were staffed by Chinese.

I happened to have a cousin in Shanghai, a wealthy civil engineer, whose firm had constructed the imposing Bund facing the river, which had to be built on piles owing to the shifting sand. He had a magnificent steam yacht called the *Olive*, on

Olive

which he made shooting expeditions up the creeks surrounding
the city, in search of snipe. During the few days I was in
Shanghai, I was able to make a trip with him.

The Chinese countryside literally teemed with people:
shooting snipe, which rise quickly, and fly low and erratically,
is a hazardous business. Inevitably, from time to time, people
unfortunately got peppered with shot, which led to long argu-
ments about the amount of damage inflicted. Attention would be
drawn, on the one hand, to the serious nature of the wounds
inflicted, and played down as mere scratches on the other.
Compromise is part and parcel of Chinese life, and after a good
deal of haggling, compensation for an agreed sum in Chinese
yuan or dollars would be paid on the spot.

On our way back to Shanghai, we had to pass under the bridge
carrying the Shanghai-Nanking railway. The yacht had a funnel,
hinged so that it could be let down when passing under a low
bridge, such as this one. My cousin came up on deck, just as we
were approaching the bridge, to find the funnel still up and no
sign of the "laodah" or steersman. He bellowed down the hatch,
and summoned him on deck, at the same time losing his temper
in pidgin English: "Master very bobbery—laodah no come
puttee funnel down—master very bobbery indeed". He was just
in time to save the funnel from being badly crushed. The sight

Two "shootie" men

and sound of an adult Westerner losing his temper in pidgin English was rather ludicrous.

We had with us two Chinese "shootie" men; the sportsman, who carries a pellet gun with a very long single barrel and practically no stock, appears to shoot from the hip, and seldom misses his target. The economics of Chinese life are such that he shoots seldom and accurately: he couldn't possibly afford to blaze away with a two barrelled gun, as we do. In North China, where the bustard, or wild turkey, has its habitat, usually in flat country with little cover, the "shootie" man is quite used to hiding inside a covered pit for several days for the chance of a certain shot.

After about a week in and around Shanghai, we set off in a 2,000 ton coastal steamer for Tientsin, the voyage being uneventful, until we reached the Taku Bar guarding the approaches to that city. The water here is shallow, and steamers have to lay off, and load and unload into barges. It was here that engagements were fought between Chinese and foreign forces in 1860, when the two Imperial summer palaces outside Peking were completely destroyed and looted, after which the foreign embassies were set up in the capital, and in 1900, when these same embassies were besieged by the Boxers (The Society of Harmonious Fists), and had to be relieved by an allied force sent up from Tientsin, which had been made into a Treaty port in 1858.

The rail journey to Peking took about two hours, and we were soon speeding along in rickshaws to the modern missionary language school on the outskirts of the city, where we had been allocated a house in the compound.

This was a school for Protestant missionaries who, since their first arrival in China in the 19th Century, had made a great contribution to the study and translation of the language. The Bible and the gospels were translated into Chinese, and in later years, when mission schools were opened and organisations like the YMCA started to appear, translations were made of more secular works. Robert Morrison, who became the interpreter for the East India Company in its closing years, was one of the earliest pioneering Protestant missionaries.

Members of the business communities in the Treaty ports seldom took the trouble to learn the language, as they could usually get by with English or pidgin English. Missionaries, however, who mostly lived in the interior and saw Chinese life at first hand, had to be proficient at least in the spoken language. If you were an evangelist, it wasn't much use trying to make converts to Christianity, if you couldn't communicate; similarly with doctors who wanted to discover patients' symptoms. Interpreters simply weren't good enough.

Here we were to live for the next 18 months, with the exception

of one of our number, who was sent home after six months with
DTs: the attractions of Peking's night life, such as it was,
coupled with a complete inability to grapple with the tones and
ideographs of the language, proved too much for him. The other
students in the school were all missionaries, but we were segre-
gated, as the requirements of our course were different. Elsewhere in the city, budding consuls and military men of various
nationalities were also learning the language, their courses
usually being of three years' duration. Most foreign students
came to Peking to learn the language: Peking Mandarin equates
with Oxford English, and is supposed to be the perfect accent.

My unforgettable first lesson went off roughly in this way.
The teacher, immaculate in grey gown, with short, black,
buttoned coat, slipper-type black shoes, and round black bonnet,
surmounted by a centrally placed red button, bowed gravely as
we met: I reciprocated, and we then entered a small cubicle with
two hard chairs in it. Not a word had been spoken, as we sat
down facing each other, when he suddenly started poking the
forefinger of his right hand several times at his chest, at the same
time uttering the word "WO" (pronounced like WAR) and
repeating it. Then, without speaking, he indicated by signs, that
I should follow suit and imitate what he had done. After I had
"warred" several times, in the same tone of voice that he had
used, he seemed satisfied that, not only did I know that "WO"
meant "I", but that I had mastered the pronunciation and the
tone of the word "WO".

He then poked his forefinger several times at my chest, at the
same time producing "NI" (pronounced like KNEE). I reciprocated, and soon convinced him that I had mastered "NI", when
suddenly a man passed by the window, which immediately set
him off pointing his forefinger in that direction, and saying "TA"
(pronounced like a light TA, or thank you). By the time I got
ready, "TA" had disappeared, but fortunately the portrait of a
man hanging on the wall came to my rescue, and I was able to
establish continuity through him.

The plurals of these three pronouns were a relatively simple
matter, as he started alternately poking his forefinger, first at
himself, and then at me, in a "let's get together" sort of way, at
the same time producing "WO MEN", "NI MEN" etc. I now
had six pronouns under my belt, and to this day do not know
whether my teacher had a word of English.

Mention has been made of "tone". In Mandarin Chinese there
are four tones. The first requires a fairly high and straight pitch
of the voice, thus — : the second, a slightly rising inflection ╱ :
the third a steeply rising inflection ╱ : the fourth a slightly falling
inflection ╲:. In many parts of South China there is not only a

multitude of dialects, but a differing variety of tones, there being no less than nine tones in Cantonese. Generally speaking, Mandarin Chinese is spoken in most of the areas north of the Yangtse, in the area of the lower Yangtse basin, and in the four Southwestern provinces of Sichuan, Yunnan, Guizhou and part of Hunan.

Chinese is monosyllabic, and the entire spoken language is based on the use of 420 monosyllables. The use of tones increases the stock of spoken meanings, but to nowhere near the total requirements of the spoken language. Take, for instance, "i" (pronounced ee), which has seven meanings in the first tone, 17 in the second, seven in the third, and no less than 38 in the fourth tone, a sum total of 69 meanings for one monosyllable. At this point you will probably throw up your hands, and say, "This language is impossible". Not so, the Chinese are past masters at overcoming the idiosyncracies of their language, though the mind boggles at the problems posed by modern technology. If you want to pursue the matter further, I can thoroughly recommend Bernard Karlgren's *Sound and Symbol in Chinese*.

The written character or ideograph conveys a meaning to the eye and mind of the reader, if that ideograph is one of which he has knowledge, but not its sound, if spoken. From this arises the curious situation, that there are erudite scholars and students of the language, who may know the meaning of 20,000 characters or ideographs, but are unable to speak a word: on the other hand, there are others, who can freely converse, with virtually no knowledge of the written language at all.

It is the written language, which has been the very cement holding together China's culture and civilisation over the centuries. It is universally understood by educated people throughout the whole country. An article in the Peking *People's Daily* conveys exactly the same meaning to a Peking man, as it does to a Canton man, but if the Peking man read the article to the Canton man, he would not understand what he was saying.

It is said that there are some 40,000 characters in the language, but many of these have long ago fallen into disuse. The requirement for students at age 16 is now 3,600, which is sufficient for reading the newspapers. A small standard dictionary might contain 4,000 characters.

The writing of characters is regarded as one of the highest forms of art: a painting will be judged, not only by the artistic merit shown in the painting itself, but also by the merit of the characters in the artist's seal or signature, or of any poem or saying he may have added to the picture.

The complexities of the Chinese language are undoubtedly a disadvantage to their people in many ways. The teaching of it

US sentry

takes up an inordinate amount of school time; its complexities make it a very difficult means of communication with other countries. Experiments have been made with the use of phonetics; a major disadvantage here is that China's vast and ancient literature was never meant to be spoken, so that students would still have to learn the characters to understand it. Many of the bigger and more complex characters have been simplified since the Communists came to power.

Whatever other problems the language presents, grammar, tenses, genders and declensions are not amongst them. Word order, however, is vitally important. A good ear and ability to imitate are useful for the spoken language—an artistic sense, patience, imagination, and a good memory for the written. The purist writes with a brush dipped in a moistened ink block; children start writing characters with a brush, and not a pen or pencil, at quite an early age, which must partly account for the Chinese being such an artistic race.

Peking was a wonderful city in which to live, particularly for a foreigner, who enjoyed many privileges. The legation quarter, scene of the siege by the Boxers in 1900, housed embassies of various countries, outside some of which were posted armed sentries; ever since the Boxer rising, the leading world powers had maintained armed forces in the capital, and indeed had the right to station troops on the Peking-Tientsin railway.

The Peking club was the Mecca where foreigners met: the two hard tennis courts there were flooded in winter, and covered with a "peng", or matting roof, for skating and ice hockey. In winter Peking suffers severely from heavy dust storms blown off the Gobi desert, the fine particles of which find their way into every nook and cranny, so that a cover over the ice was very necessary. The sun shines down from a cloudless sky for most of the year; nearly all the rainfall occurs in July and August. The temperature can rise as high as 105°F in the height of summer, and fall as low as below zero in winter.

Tame pigeons, with bamboo whistles fitted to their tails, dived down from the azure sky, making a pleasant melodious noise as they dropped. I couldn't help being reminded of them in the early days of the Second World War in France, when those death-dealing German Stukas dived down at us, emitting their blood-curdling screech. There was a "thieves' market" one could visit in the early hours of the morning, where good bargains were to be had.

The large and pretentious Peking Hotel, still in being, catered for tourists and visitors. In the tourist season, cruise ships anchored off the Taku Bar at Tientsin, and disgorged large numbers of visitors, who were often sitting ducks for the wily

Dismantling peng

dealers in the curio shops. If one wanted to dance, and had no partner, several beautiful White Russian ladies were to be found in the hotel, who were only too willing to offer their services. Emigrées, who had fled from Red Russia after the 1917 Revolution, most of them lived in Ha-Erbin in North Manchuria, or Shanghai, where they eked out a miserable existence far from their home country. I often wonder what fate has overtaken them since the fearful upheavals in China, from the time of the Japanese invasion of Manchuria in 1931, to the establishment of the People's Republic in 1949, and subsequent Communist regime.

Fascinating were the "hutungs", narrow lanes, gay with the names of the shops printed in different colours on cloth banners hung between the houses on both sides of the lanes, almost as if there was a permanent display of bunting. Too narrow for a car, hutungs could be used for rickshaws or bicycles at slow speeds. Here were the shops selling books, pictures, scrolls, curios, beads, glassware, jewellery, and in fact all those products of that astonishing patience in creative work, for which the Chinese are so renowned. Exquisite embroideries, worked with the finest stitch and a baffling array of colours, none of which clashed— intricate pieces of carved ivory—small glass snuff bottles, painted inside with a tiny brush, the tip of which is set at right angles to the brush itself. An amazing array of materials too—lacquer, jade, amber, crystal, agate, porcelain, cloisonné, rose quartz, coral, soapstone and many others. The Chinese have been making silk since the days before Christ: jade and silk were the items usually chosen by the Emperors for presentation purposes; both of them in profusion in the shops, as well as lovely brocades.

The range of goods was fantastic, none of them being sold at fixed prices. Bargaining was quite an art, and the uninitiated tourist had little idea of how to go about it. If you were a resident in Peking, and had set your mind on a valuable piece, negotiations could go on for months until the gap between the buying and selling price offers had narrowed to a point where the dealer, after you had left his shop and gone a hundred yards down the street, would come running after you, and ask you to return to his shop. He had agreed to your last offer, he would say, with extreme reluctance: you were bankrupting him, he was literally giving the piece away, and would have to cut down his rations for several weeks to pay for his mistake. Everyone, in fact, was happy: he had done pretty well, and you reckoned you had got a bargain.

On the broad boulevards of the city there was always plenty of stir and bustle, the streets and pavements being regarded as public property, and, as such, perfectly suitable places in which to transact business. With the virtual guarantee of fine weather, except in the months of July and August, there were small stands with eatables such as peanuts, small cakes, soft bread, melon seeds and the like, with the addition of ice cream and dripping water melons in summer. Barbers cut your hair on the pavements, coopers and carpenters freely plied their trades, and there was usually a peddler or two. Quite often one could see a small group of coolies squatting in a circle with a newspaper, which they contrived to read by each contributing the small stock of characters, the meaning of which they knew. Then there were the letter writers, an important feature of life in a country where the people were largely illiterate: letters could be written to the requirements of the sender for a few coppers. Rickshaw coolies were always drifting about looking for a fare, preferably a foreigner, who was adjudged likely to pay a higher rate. "Ch'e" (cart), you shouted, and several rickshaws would appear as if from nowhere. "Shang na'r?" (Where to?) would be followed by an offer by one of the coolies to take you to your stated destination for so many coppers, to be immediately capped by a lower offer from another, until rock bottom was reached. You then mounted, and the successful bidder started off, muttering to himself that he had been cheated and badly done by.

Centuries of Confucian doctrine, involving the importance of

A letter-writer

ancestor worship and filial piety, had made the observance of funeral rites a matter of protocol for every Chinese family. The size of the funeral procession depended on the wealth of the departed and his family: the catafalque could be borne aloft by no less than 128 bearers, 64 fore and aft, with numerous musicians and professional mourners dressed in white, scattering paper money about for the use of the departed in his heavenly abode, a paper cock perched on the coffin as a symbol of good luck, and the hope for many male dependants to maintain the rites of ancestor worship. At the other extreme it could be a simple ceremony for a poor coolie in a plain coffin carried aloft by eight of his relatives or companions. Protocol demanded that the eldest son of the deceased should observe three years of mourning for his deceased father.

In the depths of winter, men wearing thick felt boots, well wrapped round with straw, and armed with heavy guillotine-like knives, would cut out enormous blocks of ice from the hard frozen lakes, to be stored underground against the hot days of summer, when the filthy, dripping blocks would re-appear on trader's stands for keeping drinks, ice cream, melons and other things cool. Ice cream is called "bing ji ling", which has rather a happy ring about it for children.

The pleasures of life for most Chinese are few and simple; food and meals play a big part in them. Meet someone casually about midday and the greeting is not likely to be "How are you" or "Fine weather isn't it?" but "Have you eaten?". Peking had many restaurants, one of the specialities being Peking Duck. The bird, which has been forcibly fed, is cooked with water inside the carcass, the skin being slowly basted to a golden brown. Whole farms in the Peking area are given over to duck rearing, the sole duty of a small boy on the farm being to press a pellet of food down each duck's neck, as it waddles past him in single file. I was not to experience the etiquette and protocol attached to Chinese feasts until later, when living in the interior.

The Chinese are great lovers of the theatre, an understanding of which, in pre-revolutionary days, when all the parts on stage were played by men, required an intimate knowledge of the history and folk-lore of the country, which I lacked. Following a play in any foreign language is difficult: it was particularly so in China, having regard to the speech problems described earlier on. If an actor came on stage with a stick between his legs and a few hairs on the end of it, he was supposedly riding a horse. The face of the villain was usually painted white and the hero's red: he also often sported one or two cock pheasant's tail feathers in his hat. Blue make-up indicated that the man had an uncertain temper, and was given to outbreaks of rage. The clown usually

A team of ice-cutters

had a white patch on his face.

In spite of our growing competence with the language, I can't say we ever had much contact with the higher echelons of Chinese society, our dealings being mainly with shopkeepers, rickshaw pullers, servants and such like. This applied to the small foreign community as a whole, which lived in a kind of oasis, amongst a people whose language for the most part they didn't speak, and whose way of life was quite foreign to their own. The Chinese for their part have always tended to segregate foreigners living on Chinese soil, ever since the earliest days, when trade was exclusively conducted through Canton, and the foreign community lived on a tiny spit of land at Shameen.

The sporting activities of the foreign community consisted of skating, ice and field hockey in the winter, riding, tennis and steeplechasing on the hardy Mongolian ponies in the summer. This took place at Pao Ma Chang (The Run Horse Place), not far from Peking, where mud walls were put up for jumps, to

Ruins of the old Summer Palace

make a miniature point-to-point course. As the ponies were being got ready by the "mafoos" or grooms for the point-to-points, a man was always present with a basket on his back, which he filled with the droppings of the ponies, using a small scoop on the end of a pole to fill his basket. Nothing goes to waste in China—dung is valuable. Competitors from Tientsin also took part in the point-to-points, and twice a year there would be field hockey matches between the two communities.

Snipe shooting was another sport one could pursue, subject to the hazards mentioned earlier. One of the best places was the Yuan Ming Yuan (The Garden of Perfection and Light), better known as the old Summer Palace, just outside the northwest corner of the city, which had been utterly destroyed and looted by British and French forces in 1860, and is still a tangled mass of masonry to this day, a reminder of the head-on clash between the searching, probing, aggressive West, and the mindless, blinkered Imperial house of China. Like the Irish (the two races have much in common), the Chinese have long memories for indignities inflicted on them: no doubt the ruins are kept as a permanent reminder of the evils of imperialism. Here we gaily pottered about the reed beds and paddy fields, where once had been the gardens and pavilions of one of the finest palaces in the world, sublimely oblivious of the historical significance of the

A bag of geese

ruins about us, once the pride of those two great emperors of the Qing dynasty, Kang Xi and Qian Long.

Near a small town called Shazheng, on the river Hun Ho, up the Peking-Suiyuan railway, which ran up into Inner Mongolia, the Brent geese used to come down from Siberia in the autumn. They arrived in large numbers, spiralling down from a great height after their long journey from the frozen North—a magnificent sight. I went up there once with an officer in the U.S. Marine Corps, and we spent two nights in the village school: the panes of the windows were of rice paper, and not of glass, and in the morning, when we woke up, they were seen to be full of perforations, behind each one of which was the eye of a boy intently watching every move of the two foreign devils on their camp beds. We managed to get about a dozen geese, and there was a tremendous rush for the empty cartridge cases, when we got back to the school.

In summer time, many members of the foreign community repaired to Beidaihe on the sea northeast of Peking, quite close to where the Great Wall of China ends its 3,000 mile journey at Shanhaiguan (The mountain and sea pass). There it was just like a seaside holiday at home, with the added attraction, that there was endless domestic help to cope with the running of the trim little bungalows.

19

Bi Yun Si temple

Sun Yat Sen's Funeral Procession in Peking

Another pleasant break at a week-end in summer was a visit to one of the Buddhist temples in the Western Hills, a few miles outside Peking—Wo Fo Si (The Sleeping Buddha Temple) and Bi Yun Si (The Temple of Azure Clouds) were the most popular. You took camp beds and a picnic, and spent a night in the perfect peace and quiet of the temple, uninhabited except possibly by one or two ancient priests. The siting of important buildings in China was always dictated by a combination of "feng shui" (geomancy) and "shan shui" (choice of scenery). Bi Yun Si, a temple dating back to the fourteenth century, commanded a particularly good view of the plain round Peking: it came into prominence in 1925 as the temporary resting place of the body of the revolutionary leader Sun Yat-sen, whose remains were transferred in 1929, with great pomp and ceremony, to the new capital at Nanking, for interment on the Purple Mountain. The coffin sent by the Soviet Union arrived a fortnight late and was still in the temple. Wo Fo Si had a large, gilded, recumbent Buddha, his right arm bent to support his head, his left lying along his side.

Apart from a small body of priests conducting a weird service in the lama temple in Peking, I never saw any signs of temple worship. Most of the temples in the countryside had been turned into schools.

Seventy miles to the northwest of Peking, deep in the mountains, lay the Trappist monastery of Yang Jia Pin. It was a good

A side view of the Trappist monastery Yang Chia Pin

three-day walk, some of it in mountainous country, and I slept in the inns, as I was travelling light and alone. It was on this walk that I first made the acquaintance of the "kang", or heated bed, which I have described elsewhere.

The host, dressed in a flowing gown, the only man in the monastery permitted to converse with someone from the outside world, received me most hospitably. Both the welcome food and wine he gave me were produced by the monks themselves, who were a completely international body and subject to a very rigid discipline. I remember well being wakened by the tolling of the bell, calling them to prayers, at 3 a.m.

The monastery itself, a substantial building of stone, with a roof of corrugated iron sheeting, was of quite recent construction. Inside, the human comforts were few, the monks living in cells and the small refectory, where I ate, having a bare wooden table and benches. These were dedicated men, who lent an atmosphere of peace and tranquillity to this isolated oasis of Christianity, which made a deep impression on me.

Peking, or Cambaluc as it was known to the Mongols when their Yuan dynasty ruled China from 1222 to 1368, has been the capital since that time, apart from the short break from 1928 to 1949, when it was transferred to Nanking by Chiang K'ai Shek. Before the Mongol conquest, the capital had been in various places in the Yellow River region, such as Anyang, Ruoyang, Kaifeng, Changan (now Xian)—and even, for a short

Trappist host Frere Victor

time during the Sung dynasty, at Hangzhou in central China. It was in the Mongol court of Kublai Khan, grandson of Genghis Khan, that Marco Polo spent several years in Peking in the 13th Century. He wrote in glowing terms of the magnificence and luxury of it.

"You must know that it is the greatest palace that ever was. The hall of the palace is so large, that it could easily dine 6,000 people, and it is quite a marvel to see how many rooms there are besides. The building is altogether so vast, so rich and so beautiful, that no man on earth could design anything superior to it. The outside of the roof also is all colours, with vermilion, and yellow, and green, and blue, and other hues, which are fixed with a varnish so fine and exquisite, that they shine like crystal, and lend a resplendent lustre to the palace as seen from a great way round."

Close on the heels of Marco Polo came the Franciscan friars, to be followed by the Jesuits at the end of the 16th Century. The Jesuits, unlike the Franciscans, were not a monastic order, and did a great deal of scientific and practical work for the emperors of the Qing dynasty, until the Pope intervened in a matter of doctrine, to the great annoyance of the reigning Emperor, Kang Xi, after which Christianity was officially proscribed for many years.

The centrepiece of Peking was, and still is, the Forbidden City, now renamed The Imperial Palace. Twenty four successive Emperors reigned there, starting with Yung Lo, the third Ming Emperor (1403–1424), who built the Forbidden City in its present form, and ending with the young Pu Yi, last of the Qing dynasty, who abdicated in 1912. The Tai He Tian (The Hall of Supreme Harmony) which faces the visitor on entering the palace, was where emissaries from tributary states came with presents and tribute, and prostrated themselves, knocking the head three times on the ground, (the "ke tou"), as was demanded by protocol. It was this ceremony which the representatives of Western states refused to perform, and which, more than anything else, led to the impasse with successive Imperial courts. There are the Halls of Heavenly Tranquillity, of Peace and Longevity, of Heavenly Purity, and many others, names which conjure up visions of the Middle Kingdom, the hub of the universe, as the Chinese saw it—a kingdom which only barbarians could disturb.

Of great importance too, in China's history, is the Temple of Heaven, which lies south of the Imperial Palace, set inside two enclosures, the inner one of which is two and a half miles in circumference. The Emperors were said to enjoy the Mandate of Heaven as long as the empire was tranquil, and the harvests good. It was here that they communed with Heaven with great pomp and circumstance—at the winter solstice on the three-tiered Round Mound, and in the first month after the new year in the Imperial Heavenly Vault, near which lies the Hall of Prayer for good harvests. West of the Vault lay the Temple of Agriculture, where each year the Emperor performed the rite of ploughing the first furrow and sacrificed to bring on rain—it has since been converted into a stadium to seat 30,000 and the finest swimming pool in China.

Peking, and the area surrounding it, are very special, in that China, in spite of its long history, has few historic buildings still standing, apart from the many temples, pagodas and cave Buddhas dotted about all over the country. Most of the palaces were built of wood (the Imperial Palace is no exception), and have not stood the test of time. In Peking protocol demanded

24

Temple of Heaven

that no building could rise higher than the Imperial Palace; since 1949, however, high rise buildings have started to appear, which show up markedly in an otherwise flat city.

North of the city lies the Great Wall, known as the Wan Li Chang Cheng or the wall of ten thousand li*, and near it the Shih San Ling or Thirteen Tombs of Ming Emperors. The Great Wall, joined up from a number of subsidiary walls by the Qin Emperor Shih Huang Di during his short reign from 221 to 210 B.C., is one of the Seven Wonders of the World and is said to have been seen from the moon by the American astronauts. Such was the enormous loss of life during its construction, that it has become known as the longest cemetery in the world. Starting from the sea at Shanhaiguan, it stretches Westward for over 3,000 miles, much of its length being in a state of disrepair.

Originally conceived as a protection against the mounted barbarian raiders from the North—the Mongols, Kalmuks, Kirghiz, Tunguts, Hsiung Nu and other tribes—it has had little military significance for centuries; both the Mongol and Manchu dynasties, which ruled China, in fact came from north of it. Its psychological importance, however, is great; it represents the outer limit of China proper. It was one thing when the Japanese took over Manchuria in 1931; quite another when they opened hostilities in Hebei province in 1937—this was China proper south of the Great Wall. Today the tribes, which constantly

---

Three li equal approximately one mile.

25

The Great Wall

invaded, are for the most part in the Soviet Union, or in Outer
Mongolia, to all intents and purposes its satellite. Peking is only
400 miles distant from the nearest point on Outer Mongolia's
border.

Fired by the romance and history of this old bastion, I took
a camp bed and slept a night on one of the square towers which
are set at intervals along its length. It was a beautiful clear night,
and the Wall could be seen for miles, snaking up hill and down
dale into the far distance. Today's visitors travel from Peking in
a luxury train, a thousand at a time.

The Ming tombs are but a few miles away from the Wall,

The Summer Palace

13 of them in all, the burial vaults inside enormous round mounds with small subsidiary temples facing them, in which succeeding Emperors prayed for their ancestors. The approach is along an avenue lined with stone animals and some statues of Ming officials. Some of the halls, with their brilliant yellow tiled roofs, vie in size with those in the Imperial Palace.

Quite close to the ruined Old Summer Palace is the Yi He Yuan (The Garden where Peace is Cultivated), known today as the Summer Palace; it too was destroyed in 1860, to be restored by the Dowager Empress Zi Xi in 1888 using funds granted for the rebuilding of the Chinese Navy for that purpose. It covers an area of 660 acres, three quarters of which are taken up by the Kun Ming Lake. It was here that the Emperor Guang Xu, who tried to introduce far reaching reforms in 1898, to the fury of his aunt, was imprisoned by her in the Jade Waves Palace. There sits in the water on the northern shore of the lake a large marble boat, a kind of gesture to those who voted the grant for the rebuilding of the navy.

In April 1930, after 18 months of language study and the enjoyment of all that Peking had to offer a foreigner, the four of us got our marching orders—one to Hankow on the Yangtse, one to Mukden, the capital of Manchuria, one to the new capital of Nanking and me to Shijiazhuang (The village of the House

27

An ancient Morris six-wheeler at the Great Wall

of Shih), a railway junction on the Peking-Hankow railway about 150 miles south of Peking. Spread about as we were in this vast country, I have never seen any of my three companions again to this day.

The social life and niceties of Peking would soon be a thing of the past, as we faced the sterner, harsher realities of commercial life. Our spoken Mandarin had come on quite well and the best of us probably knew the meaning of between 1,500 and 2,000 characters—enough to read simple newspaper articles with the help of a dictionary.

Were we going to be swallowed up and lose our identity amongst China's teeming millions? What were we doing here anyway? Did one carry a gun to deal with bandits or rely on bluff? Yes, it was an exciting prospect, but faced, I am bound to say, with mixed feelings.

II
The North China Countryside, 1930—1932

The train journey to Shijiazhuang across the flat North China plain in Hebei province is unforgettable; Hebei, in which the large city of Tientsin is situated, has a population of about the same size as that of Great Britain. It was the month of April; field work was in full swing; the ground seemed black with people, and one felt almost smothered by a blanket of human beings. Wheat, maize, millet, sorghum (also called kaoliang) and cotton are the main crops in this part of China, which, owing to its climate, cannot produce the two, or even three, crops a year considered quite normal in the sub-tropical areas of South China. Some rice is grown, but it is not a staple crop; peanuts are increasing, and some fruit and nuts are grown in the more hilly parts.

The highly labour intensive agriculture in China has been called "garden farming"; the plots were certainly small, as were the areas devoted to any one crop: a peasant's holding could be anything from half an acre upwards. Many peasants owned no land at all, and rented from a landlord, who provided the tools and took up to fifty per cent of the crop: others worked for a landlord for a straight wage. The rate of interest on loans at two and a half per cent per month, or 30 per cent a year, was extortionate. The government was said to be starting up co-operatives, which would provide loans at lower rates of interest.

Tools and traction were very primitive—wooden ploughs, drawn by oxen, horses, mules or even donkeys. Artificial fertilizers were practically unknown; the home-produced manures were made up from human ordure, pig manure and any collected animal droppings, sometimes mixed in with a clover crop grown for that purpose. Crops were cut with hand sickles, and threshed by hand on winnowing floors in the villages. Irrigation was a laborious process, the water being drawn up from wells by hand-operated windlasses and tipped into the irrigation ditches, on which men worked treadmills with their feet, to keep the water moving over the dead flat ground. The peasant lived very near subsistence level, his livelihood closely bound up with the climate, and the amount of rainfall. Eighty

An irrigation windlass

five per cent of China's vast population lived in the countryside, most of them directly engaged in agriculture.

Little broke the monotony of the dead flat plain, except the mud brown villages, a river or stream, groups of conical shaped grave mounds, and an occasional small temple or pagoda. When the crops began to show, the whole area looked like a patchwork quilt, owing to differences in the size of holdings and the varied nature of the crops. None of the land was enclosed, none of it wasted. Cows or sheep grazing on pastures were not to be seen. There were practically no trees; although China is rich in coal, fuel in the countryside has always been a problem, which explains the waferlike thinness of Chinese cooking utensils.

On some of the conical grave mounds, silver imitation paper money could be seen, put there by relatives at the spring festival of qing ming, when it was customary for families to pray at the graves of their ancestors. Centuries of ancestor worship have created extraordinary rites connected with death: a man's coffin may rest for months in a room of his house, although his imminent death is not expected; and again his dead body in the coffin might remain unburied for weeks, until geomancy decided on the most propitious date and place of burial. Pearls, jade and gold were said to preserve the human body after death—hence the famous funeral suit made of jade squares, which has been shown in Chinese art exhibitions.

Roads seemed hardly to exist, the many bicycles one saw finding their way along tracks through the cultivated fields. Electricity and telephones were beginning to appear: anyone who could tap the former did so, as and when an opportunity arose, while the manner of erecting telephone wires was astonishing, the poles for the most part being crooked branches stuck into the ground, any projecting eminence also being used to support the wires, when available. Between main centres served by roads, there were some crotchety buses, which frequently broke down.

The Peking-Hankow railway was in a deplorable condition. Trains hardly ever ran to time: a fit man riding a bicycle could literally keep up with most of them, except possibly "The Express", which ran four times weekly in each direction. Some of the sleepers were made from willow trees bordering the track: pillars of the bridges were sometimes piles of sleepers arranged criss-cross fashion, the whole structure groaning, as the train crossed it at a snail's pace. Ticket collection on the passenger trains was quite arbitrary: on the goods trains, on which you also travelled, non-existent. Woe betide the man who rode on the roof of a box-car with a fat man in front of him: he was bound to be swept off in a tunnel. Every train, whether goods

Travelling conditions on Ping Han Railway

Chengtai locomotive

or passenger, was crowded to the roof with human beings, most of them laden with baskets, pots and pans, bedding, song birds in cages and even fowls or ducks. Locomotives continually broke down: as one uttered a sigh of relief, that the train was about to start again, the locomotive would suddenly puff away again to the repair sheds.

Ping Han Express

Shijiazhuang, with a population of some 10,000, was a railway junction for Taiyuan, the capital of the adjoining province of Shanxi. The small gauge Zhengtai railway, for which it was the base, was built by the French, who still maintained a staff of 15 of their nationals at Shijiazhuang to run it. It was due to be handed over to the Chinese in the near future, if the necessary funds were forthcoming for its purchase. The efficiency and good timekeeping of this railway were in marked contrast to the Pinghan, run by the Chinese, probably because the French were able to keep it out of the hands of the warring factions in the civil wars.

Life for a young foreigner in China's interior was strange, until one grew accustomed to the environment, and the fact that one was virtually cut off from the outside world, news of which was scarce, and usually out of date; wireless and transistors had hardly made their appearance in this part of the world; my vocabulary of Chinese characters was limited, which made reading the Chinese papers a laborious business.

The local foreign community consisted of my boss, an elderly Englishman, and the 15 Frenchmen, one of whom professed to be a keen shot. I had a shotgun and we made a foray together, which consisted mostly of looking up trees for thrushes. "Vite, vite, M. Logan, regardez les deux grives la bas". He got two—I couldn't bring myself to fire at them.

Up country there were missionaries in most of the larger, and some of the smaller centres, whom I always made a point of visiting, regardless of their denomination. The Roman Catholics

33

Zhenting Roman Catholic Cathedral

had been in China a good deal longer than the Protestants; their churches were usually substantial buildings of brick or stone, surrounded by a wall, within which they grew much of their own produce. They were more closely identified with the communities in which they lived than the Protestants, who tended to combine evangelism with the healing of the sick, and did not have such pretentious churches, though they did have some first class hospitals.

The Chinese may have had people in their history prepared to die as martyrs for the Buddhist or Taoist faiths—if so, I have never heard of them. Confucianism represented a philosophy and a way of life, and never pretended to be a religion. In short, the Chinese have never been a deeply religious people, their beliefs often being skin deep, liable to change and greatly influenced by secular considerations. There is the story of a young Christian Chinese acolyte, who was sent out to distribute religious tracts to the inhabitants of a small town. A few days later, a number of people in the town appeared to be wearing plasters on boils on their necks, which the young acolyte had been prescribing and selling as cures and which, in fact, were bits of the tracts he had been sent out to distribute. All this is is not to say that the missionary effort was in vain: many sincere Chinese Christians died for their faith at the time of the Boxer rising: many notable Chinese became converts to Christianity, notably Chiang K'ai-shek.

At a small, inaccessible place in the mountains in West Hebei, called Lingqiu, I had my only awkward meeting with a missionary, a Norwegian Protestant lady. I knocked, and handed in my card in the usual way: she looked at it, glared at me balefully, and said, "If you believed in Jesus, you would not do such things." It was an unhappy occasion: I slouched off, muttering that I knew of no passage in the Bible which condemned tobacco. How could there be?

Occasionally one might meet a foreign representative of the two major oil companies operating in China, the Standard Oil Co. of New York, abbreviated to Socony, and the Asiatic Petroleum Co., a subsidiary of Shell. The paraffin, for which they had a large market, was supplied in tall, rectangular, silver coloured, sealed tins, which were greatly prized as empties, for use as buckets or containers for carrying fluids. Frequently one met a Chinese walking along at a short, steady trot, carrying two such tins, one at each end of his carrying pole.

China was heavily in debt to foreign powers, and had to meet the interest on various foreign loans, arranged partly to pay indemnities, after defeats such as that in the Sino-Japanese War of 1894/5, or after rioting involving the lives of foreigners, such as the Boxer Rising in 1900, and partly to finance such developments as railway construction. In many cases the interest was secured on the revenues of the Customs service and the Salt Gabelle, a government organisation controlling the production and sale of salt, an important ingredient of the country's foodstuffs. The Customs service had gone further and developed the system of lighthouses on the coasts, and the Post Office. Both these organisations were still employing foreigners, and two of them were stationed in Taiyuanfu, one a Dane in the Post Office, and the other an Englishman in the Salt Gabelle. The only other foreigner in Taiyuan, not a missionary, was employed by Yan Xi Shan as an engineer in his arsenal.

Constant travelling came to be the main ingredient of my life, as the depots and offices were widely scattered. One often went on foot, even if officially riding in a cart, or mule litter, or sitting sideways on to the pusher of a wheelbarrow. Apart from communications between main centres, there were virtually no roads, and no signposts—one simply asked one's way from one village to the next. Houses in the villages were made of sundried bricks—occasionally one might see a house of kiln dried bricks or stone, possibly the landlord's. Streets were simply of tamped earth, with no sidewalks. Pigs ran helter skelter down the streets, and hens in and out of the houses, the former much leaner and more athletic than ours. Usually there were one or more mangy looking dogs (called wonks by foreigners): it was considered ominous if the wonks failed to bark at you as a foreigner, and meant that you were on the way to becoming assimilated into the Chinese way of life. I usually wore shorts in summer, which intrigued small boys, who would come running up, feel the hairs on my knees and shout delightedly, "Qi guai! Qi guai!"—how odd! how odd! The Chinese have fewer hairs on their bodies than we have and their hair appears to grow more slowly: very few Chinese men have to shave every day—sometimes only twice, or even once a week.

If one had no camp bed, sleeping in the inns meant securing a place on the kang, a brick built platform raised some two feet above floor level, with flues beneath to heat it in winter time, when the Chinese in the country wore thick padded clothing, which they seldom changed. They would spend the early hours of the night roasting hot, as the heat from the kang was at its maximum: you, as a foreigner, took off the clothes worn during the day, went to sleep, cosily warm, on the kang, only to wake up freezing cold in the early hours of the morning, as the fire below had died out. Sleeping on the kang was a communal affair, with all and sundry taking a share of the available space. In South China, where there is little or no heat requirement, I understand you sleep on boards mounted on trestles. In North China it was important to examine your boots before putting them on in the morning as scorpions like the moist warmth of the empty human boot, and can be lethal.

Most of the population in the countryside lived in scattered villages, the smallest unit of administration responsible to the provincial or central government being the xian, headed by a district magistrate. It dealt with the administration of justice, the maintenance of law and order, and the collection of taxes in villages within its orbit of responsibility, and equated roughly with a county town in Great Britain. Each village elected or chose a "di bao", who was the link with the xian, and agreed the amount of land tax to be levied on the village.

Chinese government officials had traditionally always been underpaid, it being generally understood that, by various means, they should augment their meagre incomes at the expense of those they administered. As a result, the country people have always feared officialdom, and steered clear of it, settling their disputes and quarrels in the villages themselves, as far as possible. If a case arose, which could not be settled at village level, and had to go to the xian, woe betide any villager who got a prison sentence from the district magistrate. The length of his stay in prison, and the quantity and quality of the food he got while there, depended largely on the length of his purse.

The system had been in operation for centuries, and took no account of the functions normally associated with local government, such as education, health, hygiene, sanitation, upkeep of roads and streets, and so forth. No officially sponsored elections had ever been held in xian or village: people were simply chosen by popular acclaim, usually from the ranks of the landlords and gentry. Before I left, an experiment had been started by students trained abroad, to make a modern xian at Dingzhou in Hebei province, this to be a model for the whole country. There were already faint stirrings of their work to be seen, in the shape of crude signposts on the roads, street names and elementary public lavatories. Chiang K'ai-shek had nearly succeeded in uniting his country: China was beginning to bestir and modernise herself: the Japanese invasion of Manchuria and subsequent war put paid to all that.

It has been frequently said, that the Chinese have always been a democratic people, and that the villages could be compared to self-governing republics, the craft guilds and the clan system being well able to stand up against officialdom. The leaders of the village communities were usually the landlords and gentry; by definition the landlord was usually the owner of a considerable acreage of land, the gentry were those with superior

37

education, but not necessarily owners of land. The choice of leaders was a matter for the villagers themselves: there was no question of organised elections supervised by the xian. This laissez-faire system may have worked well in Imperial days, but, at a time of constant civil war and banditry, led to serious difficulties, as more cohesion between different communities was required. The beginning of class warfare, and of the struggle between master and man, aggravated by Russian influence in the 1920s, began to undermine the authority of landlords and gentry, whose leading role had hitherto been looked on as a matter of course.

The clan system operated in many of the villages, members of the clan, who were all of the same name, being responsible for the deeds and misdeeds of all its other members. Corporate responsibility had been part and parcel of the Chinese system of justice for generations: this frequently led to misunderstandings with foreigners. In a celebrated case at Canton, where the East India Co. had a monopoly of British trade, a Chinese had met his death at the hands of a foreign sailor; the Chinese authorities demanded that the culprit should be handed over to them and, on being told that he was not available or could not be found, demanded that another sailor of the same nationality be handed over—to almost certain death by strangulation.

There was much to be done by those in authority in the villages. For many centuries civil service examinations had been held for pupils of above average ability from all over the country; successful candidates aspired to posts as officials in government service. In a country noted for its admiration of scholars, success in these examinations was regarded as a supreme achievement. They were the only examinations held under the auspices of the central government. Until the beginning of educational reform in 1905 and the introduction of a much wider range of subjects, it was left to the villages to educate the children, temples, deserted as centres of religion, being often used as school buildings. Teachers were appointed by the villages and paid for out of village funds. By 1917 it was estimated that about 10 per cent of pupils were being educated in government schools. Girls for the most part got no formal education at all under the old system. Confucius said of women, "She may take no step on her own motion and may come to no conclusion on her own deliberation, for she yields obedience to the instruction of men." Many of the older women in the villages had bound feet, which restricted their movement and made them walk on the heel and big toe, but binding was recently made illegal.

In the cities, the emancipation of women had already begun. Increasing numbers of students were going overseas to foreign

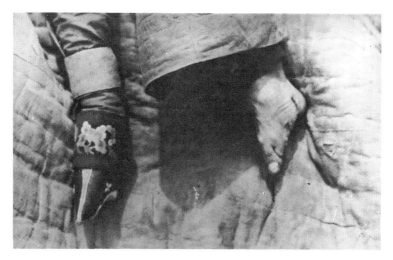

Bound feet

universities, particularly in Japan and the USA, and there were many girls among them.

Protection services had to be organised in the villages, both to keep out bandits and to protect the crops at harvest time. Night watchmen were appointed to go the rounds of the village, beating a gong. Some of the villages maintained a kind of militia, armed with swords or old fashioned rifles. Some had mud walls round them which were constantly in need of repair. Against a descent by the military, in any number, the villagers were powerless; soldiers demanded food and shelter for themselves, and fodder for their animals—another imposition on the already overburdened villagers, for none of it was paid for.

Brawling and drunkenness are not common in China, but the village elders did have minor misdemeanours, petty theft and family quarrels to deal with: everything possible was done to settle matters at the village level: a favourite punishment was to make the miscreant provide a feast for the injured parties, or indeed the whole village.

Life in the villages was not a bed of roses, as there were few amenities. Plays were popular, either staged by the villagers themselves or by a travelling troupe. More than once I saw a Punch and Judy show, and a pageant on stilts. Visits to neighbouring markets, to buy or sell produce, were a welcome break. Most important were harvest time and the New Year. To celebrate the first there was a village feast, and many debts would be paid off, as there was more money about.

Pageant on stilts

Families would gather a week before New Year to worship the kitchen god, an image in the house, the mouth of which was smeared with molasses, so that nothing but good should be reported about the family on high; on the last day of the old year, he was welcomed back to the sound of crackers. All debts were traditionally settled at New Year time.

Some serious crimes were, of course, outwith the competence of the villages, or indeed sometimes of the xian. The two most heinous crimes in the old China were treason and parricide, both of which merited death by the thousand cuts, the victim being slowly dismembered while still alive, until the coup de grace was administered by plunging a dagger in his heart.

Punishments were inflicted to a set scale, to fit the crime. The most lenient was a number of strokes from a bamboo, varying from 10 to a 100, according to the seriousness of the crime. Next came banishment, with or without hard labour, for a specified period, probably to Yili in Xinjiang, near the Russian border. Lastly, the death penalty, the nature of which also varied according to the crime—by strangulation, decapitation or the thousand cuts already described.

Decapitation was still being practised during my stay in China. Great efforts were being made in Shanxi province to stamp out the curse of opium smoking. From time to time a wretched addict, his hands tied behind his back, and a narrow board, on

Feng Yu Xiang

41

Yan Xi Shan

which his crime was advertised, stuck up behind it, was transported in an open cart to a point below and just outside the city wall. News of the execution had obviously been broadcast, as large crowds were sauntering up and down on the city wall overlooking the place of execution, fanning themselves and in their Sunday best. The wretch was unloaded from the cart, made to kneel facing the crowd, and was then decapitated by a single blow from a heavy sword, said to contain a column of mercury in its handle to facilitate the follow-through. It was quite a short time after this, that I saw a man riding a bicycle in the country outside Taiyuan, which, to my utter amazement, had two human heads on its carrier, presumably being sent for display on some city wall, as a deterrent to others. It was all very medieval.

Overshadowing all else in pre-revolutionary China were the civil wars, the destruction and suffering which accompanied them, and the economic consequences of large numbers of men under arms, who were non-productive.

Two warring generals were involved in the area in which I worked—Yan, who had virtually ruled Shansi province since the Manchu abdication in 1912, and was finally ousted by the Communists in the 1940s, and Feng, known variously as the Christian general and the Red general, and one of the most colourful figures on the Chinese scene.

Yan Xi Shan, at one time a student of military affairs in Japan, was a born fence-sitter, who kept his power by playing one warlord off against another: he was helped in this by the geography of Shanxi province, which is well protected by mountains, and relatively easy to defend. He was a mixture of idealism and a wish to improve the lot of his people, coupled with personal ambition and self aggrandisement. Like all the warlords, he suffered from a constant and chronic shortage of funds to pay his troops, which inhibited his grandiose plans for the economic rehabilitation of his province, and saddled the people in it with an unbearable level of taxation, which included "likin", a form of transit tax, which has always been popular in China, as it can be levied and stopped with little difficulty. Cut off from the seaports, and thus from safe access to foreign arms, he built a considerable arsenal at Taiyuan, which turned out rifles, ammunition, and hand grenades, but no heavy weapons, and which was an added financial burden to his hard pressed people. He is said to have accumulated a large personal fortune, escaped to Taiwan and died there at the age of 77 in 1960.

Feng Yu Xiang, born in 1882, the son of a soldier, was a very different type of general. He had come up the hard way through the ranks, was a good leader of men, and ended up as one of the leading contenders for power, only to be defeated by Chiang K'ai-shek in October 1930, just after I had started work in the interior. He came in contact with Christianity at quite an early age, believed initially in the Christian doctrine, and encouraged his officers and men to become converts to the faith. He is reputed to have carried out mass baptisms with a hose pipe!

When quite a young man, he listened to a sermon by a Christian missionary, who said, "If someone strikes you on your right cheek, turn and offer him your left; if he takes your outer clothing, do not hesitate to offer him your inner clothing too." Following this sermon, Feng and a friend decided to walk off with a table out of the church. When the missionary accused them of stealing the table, and asked for it back, Feng replied that he should be offering them the chairs and benches as well!

In his early days, Feng was a sincere Christian believer: he did all he could to suppress opium smoking, gambling and prostitution, and, in this respect, anticipated the puritanical measures of the Communists later; in practical matters the dividing line between Christianity and Communism is not as great as it might seem to be. His troops were better disciplined than most: it was strange to hear the lusty singing of "Onward Christian soldiers" and other Christian hymns in the middle of China. He, too, was constantly short of funds, and, when in dire financial straits, did not hesitate to print his own currency notes, and foist them off on the people.

During the later war against Japan he did everything in his power to arouse the people in their fight against the invader, and was the only one of the pre-revolutionary warlords to be given a state burial by the Communist Party.

The seeds of civil war were first sown in the Taiping rebellion, which lasted from 1850 to 1864, and was dedicated to the overthrow of the Manchu dynasty, the resources of which it stretched to the limit. The traditional military resources of the Qing dynasty, in the shape of provincial troops, were quite inadequate to deal with a rising on this scale, and immense powers had to be delegated to the generals, Zheng Guo Fan and Li Hong Zhang: from this time onwards, it came to be realised that power in China rested with the man who commanded the best and biggest army.

After the abdication of the Manchu dynasty in 1912, and the subsequent declaration of the Republic of China, Yuan Shih Kai had the strongest and most efficient army, with which he was able, more or less, to keep the peace, particularly in North China, until his death in 1916. From then on, the country became a prey to warring factions. It had been the original intention of the revolutionaries to establish the capital of the new republic at Nanking, a plan thwarted by Yuan Shi Kai, who kept it at Peking, which then became the focal point for all the wheeling and dealing between the warring factions, until Chiang K'ai-shek more or less united the country in 1928, and did transfer the capital to Nanking.

War damage

Large scale pitched battles between the warring factions were few and far between, although many walled cities in North China still bear the marks of concentrated artillery fire. The Chinese are not by nature a warlike race, believing more in the virtues of guile and bluff to achieve their ends, rather than in military confrontation: the warlord's strength and bargaining power lay more in the number of men and the size of the territory he controlled, than in the military competence of his subordinates. Only Chiang K'ai-shek, who had been the commandant of the military academy at Whampoa, near Canton, where he had the help of Russian military advisers, had anything approaching a modern army.

The warlords tended to stick to the railways, which gave them and their armies mobility: there was a limit to the duration of their stay in any one place, as they usually fed off the population. One warlord in North China had a complete armoured train, another a train of luxury coaches, in which he housed his senior staff and concubines. The men, horses and mules mostly rode in open railway trucks. Medical services were conspicuously absent, which was not surprising, as the number of qualified doctors in China at this time worked out at about one to 90,000 of the population. I once saw 30 wounded men laid out on the bottom of an open, metal, 40-ton freight car, in the searing heat of midsummer, only protected from the sun by some flimsy matting. They were completely stoical and expressionless, as is always the way with the Chinese in suffering.

The soldiers came mostly from the ranks of the hungry and jobless, and were usually ill-disciplined, under-equipped, and poorly turned out. Their small pay was sometimes months in arrears, and they were then driven by hunger and desperation to join the ranks of the bandits: the dividing line between the two was a fine one: in theory the soldier was paid by his unit, the bandit lived by robbing others.

A profitable side-line for the bandits was the bandit insurance society, which levied a toll on travellers about to enter a bandit-infested area. You were politely stopped at what looked like a toll house and requested to hand over a dollar or two, in return for a safe conduct pennant, which you stuck up in a prominent place on your cart or conveyance. Failure to pay the premium resulted in robbery and unpleasantness along the road, and it was safer to take the line of least resistance, although the foreigner, often suspected of carrying arms and not hesitating to use them, was less likely to be robbed than a Chinese.

Historically the soldier has always been rated low in the social scale in China. "Nails are not made of good iron, nor soldiers of good men" the saying went. Merchants in the cities, and peasants in the countryside, dreaded a descent by soldiers. In the cities, buildings would be requisitioned for barracks, merchants could be clapped into gaol, if they did not subscribe to the upkeep of the troops, foodstuffs would be commandeered without payment, and the town would be rent by the shouts and cries of the soldiers, and the singing of Christian hymns, if they were Feng's men. Trains could be commandeered on sight, and the passengers ejected: men and boys could be conscripted in thousands. It was much the same in the countryside, on a smaller scale.

Taxation had reached such a pitch in some areas, that they had been collected five, or even more, years in advance of the due date. The whole burden of thousands of these unproductive soldiers lay like a millstone round the necks of the common people, who had no resources to fall back on in an emergency, such as drought or flood. In days gone by, reserves of grain had been stockpiled in certain places against emergencies—bad government and the warlords had emptied the granaries.

And yet, in spite of all the chaos, banditry and poverty, it was in 1928, the year I came to China, that, on the face of it, the country was more united than it had been at any time since the declaration of the Republic in 1912. Chiang K'ai-shek had defeated the Northern warlords operating from Peking: the capital had been transferred to Nanking: the growing Communist threat, inspired and motivated by the Soviet Union, had been defeated in the previous year, and had gone underground: Manchuria, under Zhang Xue Liang, had agreed to accept the

Young Chiang K'ai Shek

47

rule of Nanking. Finally, in 1930, a revolt by Yan Xi Shan and Feng Yu Xiang was easily suppressed.

But it was not to be. The faint stirrings of a new order derived from foreign influence: Chiang K'ai-shek, also supported by foreign funds, was first and foremost a militarist, who had indicated the belief, shared by other warlords, that political power derived from military force alone. An ever-increasing share of the budget was devoted to military purposes: the promised reforms, which were long overdue, never materialised.

There followed the Japanese invasion of Manchuria in 1931, the miraculous escape from encirclement of the Red Army in Shangxi province, followed by the Long March to northwest China in 1934, and finally the Japanese invasion of China proper in 1937. Chiang K'ai-shek was faced with the dilemma of whether to use his forces to contain Communism or fight off the invaders. His failure to offer more than token resistance to the Japanese, coupled with his inability to introduce long overdue reforms, played into the hands of the Communists.

The long looked-for peace and unity had not materialised: the Chinese had to endure another 17 years of war and suffering, culminating in the declaration of the new "People's Republic of China" in Peking on October 1, 1949.

The Far East has a magnetic attraction for anyone who has spent some time in it. I have visited China three times, in 1974, 1977 and 1980, and hope later to describe the scope and extent of the enormous changes which have taken place since the advent of Communist rule.

III
Smoking

MOST people in Western countries, even those with but a passing interest in China, associate opium with it—and rightly so, for it was the smuggling of opium which bedevilled the relationship between China and the West for many years.

The Arabs first introduced opium to China in the eighth century AD, when it was known as a soporific used for medicinal purposes. The importation of tobacco from the Philippines followed much later in 1620; it was soon found that the addition of a little opium to the smoke had a pleasant, soothing effect; from this it was but a short step to the smoking of pure opium. Both were denounced by the Ming dynasty in 1629, and were prohibited on pain of death by an imperial decree of the Qing dynasty in 1729. The decree, however, had little effect, as the officials, or mandarins, who profited from the trade in both commodities, turned a blind eye to the traffic.

By the 1830s smuggling of opium, mostly from India, but some from Turkey, had reached such proportions that the government became alarmed at the drain of silver out of the country to pay for it. The attempt to stop it led to the Opium War of 1840 and to the subsequent legalisation of its import by the Treaty of Tientsin in 1858; by 1867 it was accounting for 67 per cent of all the imports, from which time the home grown product, mostly from the province of Yunnan and Southwestern China, began to take the place of the imports; by 1905 opium accounted for only seven and a half per cent of imports.

By 1915 there was some semblance of control of the drug; imports from India had ceased entirely and 15 out of 18 provinces had stopped growing the poppy. The breakdown of central government, however, and the rise of warlordism, soon started to increase home production again, the warlords, always short of money, being not slow to realise its attractions as a source of revenue. In 1924 China became the world's biggest opium producer with a total of 25 million pounds, against the mere two million pounds produced in India.

The opium addict, miserable and emaciated from smoking the drug, found the greatest difficulty in withstanding the craving for it; a heavy putrid smell permeated his whole house. Its cultivation and use, except for medicinal purposes, have been banned by the present government.

Until the arrival of the cigarette, the Chinese had smoked tobacco in a pipe with a small metal bowl and a long straight stem, crushing a small quantity of dry tobacco leaf into the bowl, a practice that many of them still have today.

The modern cigarette has its origin with the South American Aztecs, who used to roll up shredded tobacco in a tobacco leaf, light it, and inhale the smoke up their noses. In Europe, pipe-smoking was popular, until hand made cigarettes, mostly of Turkish tobacco, made their appearance. It was the First World War which popularised Virginia cigarettes in Europe: it was the invention of the cigarette-making machine which brought about mass production, and it was at this point that the British American Tobacco Co. Ltd. appeared on the scene in China, pioneering the sale of cigarettes by simply lighting up and handing over lighted cigarettes to the locals. By the time I arrived in China in 1928, there were cigarette factories in Shanghai, Hankow, Tientsin and Hongkong, a sales and administrative organisation throughout the country, and a department devoted to the improvement of tobacco seed varieties and farming methods.

On the adminstrative and sales side, China was divided into seven divisions, each with a divisional manager, who was responsible for a number of territories staffed and managed by Chinese employees. Conditions in the country had deteriorated so much, that most of the foreign employees, who spoke virtually no Chinese, were withdrawn into the treaty ports. Foreign supervision in future was to be exercised by a much smaller number of younger men well versed in the language. Our little party of four, who had graduated in the language, were the first fruits of the new policy.

Our headquarters in Shijiazhuang (sometimes also known as Zhengding) were in a large, foreign-style building inside a walled compound near the station. An elderly English divisional manager was in residence, as was Mr. Cui, the senior Chinese distributor, sometimes known as the comprador. They both met me at the station, the latter in his flowing, grey gown and short, black jacket, which were the typical garments of the more affluent Chinese at the time: he wore black slipper-type shoes.

Protocol always has been, and still is, of the essence of Chinese life and behaviour and one didn't just shoot out one's right hand in a hearty manner, and say, "How'dy, Mr. Cui". One bowed gravely, grasping one's two hands together, and slowly pumping them up and down, while he did likewise, at the same time asking the ritual questions, which such an occasion demanded, such as, "Are your mother and father both well? Did you come the whole

Shijiazhuang office

of the way from Peking by train, or some of it by Peking cart? You must be very tired after the journey?'' These formalities over, we repaired to the headquarters, about half a mile from the station, which served both as residence and office, and which, with its garden, occupied about a couple of acres.

When on the subject of protocol, it should be mentioned that there are formalities on departure, as well as on arrival. As before, you start pumping both hands up and down, and try to say farewell on reaching the door, a procedure which is totally ignored by your host, who steps out to accompany you. At this point, you say in an agitated voice, "Bu song, Bu song" or "Don't accompany, don't accompany", to which he pays little attention, until he has reached a point, beyond which he has decided to accompany you no longer. The further he accompanies you, the more "face" you are acquiring.

The roomy offices were well staffed, as jobs with foreign companies were much sought after: they were well paid, you could rely on getting your salary regularly, and you had an opportunity to learn English, the lingua franca of the treaty ports.

At the side of each desk on the floor was a large, round spittoon, as the Chinese all had the habit of spitting, each ejection being preceded by a harsh, raucous clearing of the throat. On each desk were small circular tea-cups without handles, each with a saucer, to be placed on the cup to keep the

Mr Cui

tea warm: it was the sole duty of a diminutive tea-boy to dispense the tea during working hours. Outside in the compound there was a hard tennis court, and I well remember, after one exhausting single with a member of the staff, coming into the building, unkempt and pouring with sweat. Mr. Cui accosted me, and said, "Wasting strength, I see, Mr. Lo." Shorts, hairy legs, and a sweaty shirt offended the sense of decorum expected by the older generation of Chinese. In any case, why waste strength built up by good food? It was uneconomical.

You will notice that I had been addressed as "Mr. Lo", which raises the knotty problem of Chinese names given to foreigners. Every Chinese has a "xing", or surname, which comes first, and a "ming zi" or personal name, which comes second, and usually, but not always, has two characters or ideographs. If, for instance, you are discussing a Mr. Wu with a friend in his absence, the friend may ask, "Which Mr. Wu?" and you may reply, saying, "Mr. Wu Deng Xue", identifying Mr. Wu by his personal names and, if necessary, by the ideographs relevant to these names.

Foreigners are given Chinese names, which are the nearest sound equivalent of their foreign name to one, or more, of the 420 monosyllables forming the sound base of the Chinese language. Herein lies the rub, for any one of the monosyllables can have 20, or 30, meanings, and the choice of your Chinese names in ideographs can be an arbitrary one. I was particularly fortunate in that the two monosyllables, LO and GAN, making up my name, were given ideographs meaning "a net for catching birds" and "efficient" respectively. What better title could an ambitious business man possibly want? For the sound of LO, there are 19 different meanings in my medium-size dictionary— a note in singing, plunder, ecstasy, the glare on the water, scrofula, a deep open basket without cover or handle, silk thread, a net for catching birds, naked, to fall, parasitic and creeping plants, slaves, a couch, a patrol, a gong, a black horse with a white mane, a white or cream-coloured horse with a black mane, a mule, and naked (second time). I won't trouble you with the 22 meanings associated with the sound of GAN. Suffice it that my patron, who named me so suitably in the first place, might have had a grudge against me and produced "A cream coloured horse with a black mane—delicious" or even "Naked ulcers"!

If, therefore, for business or other reasons, you want your foreign name and address on one side of a visiting card, and your Chinese name on the other, you have been warned. The Chinese have an acute sense of humour, and can play you a dirty trick!

My boss, in his 50s, came from Stafford, and had had long experience in China, as was evident from the fact that he often

Unloading No I cigarettes

wore a long, embroidered, Chinese gown, a sure sign that he was being assimilated into the oriental way of life. Throughout their long history, the Chinese have readily assimilated foreigners, not least the two foreign dynasties—the Yuan or Mongol and the Qing or Manchu—who ruled them. It was just as well that he was a bachelor, as life for a white woman in Shijiazhuang would not have been very exciting, though he might have aspired to a concubine, as did all the 15 Frenchmen, who lived in the town and ran a local branch railway. Life for a white woman married to a Chinese was far from plain sailing, as the keeping of a concubine, as well as a wife, was considered perfectly normal. There was a Chinese professor at the Taiyuan University in the neighbouring province of Shanxi, who had an English wife, and openly espoused a concubine, to the near mental derangement of the wife, who tried to leave him. She had lost her British citizenship by marrying a foreigner, and could only return to the United Kingdom, and stay there for a long enough period to become a naturalised British citizen.

I spent the first three weeks at Shijiazhuang studying the geography of the Luhan division, its communications, the state of our trade and that of our competitors, the names and locations of our seven territories and any other sub-offices, and the organisation of our dealers. The company's cigarettes were packed in

A mule litter

tin-lined wooden cases containing 50,000, the total sales of which, over the whole divisional area, which comprised the Hebei and Shanxi provinces and parts of Henan and Shaanxi, fluctuated between 6,000 and 10,000 cases, or 300–500 million cigarettes a month. Goods were shipped in every conceivable sort of conveyance; payment for them was mostly through bank drafts, although the company occasionally had to collect specie in the shape of silver dollars. Communications for the traveller varied from the Peking-Hankow Railway, mentioned in the previous chapter, which more or less bisected the area from North to South, to a wheelbarrow with an enormous centre wheel, on each side of which was a narrow platform, one for the passenger and the other for his luggage, so that you sat sideways on to the pusher of the barrow: when used for heavier freight, such as two wooden cases of cigarettes, there would probably be a puller on a rope, as well as a pusher.

In the mountainous areas, where rocky tracks were the order of the day, the mule litter was usually the preferred method of travel. This consisted of a couple of poles slung between two mules, a blanket or two stretched across and fixed to the poles, and an overhead matting awning fixed above, to keep off the sun. The whole contraption, which swayed from side to side with the movement of the mules, resembled a travelling hammock. I

Two views of the Peking Cart

preferred to walk alongside, as the sickening farts of the mules, largely fed on chopped straw, were a disincentive to riding in the litter.

The Peking Cart, supposedly the Rolls Royce of country travel, was an abomination, with narrow iron shod wheels, and no springs: it boasted a nicely fitted canopy, which gave it a spurious appearance of class, and was pulled by a single pony or mule, the harness usually in tatters, and held together by rope or string: it also suffered from the same disadvantage as the mule litter, already mentioned.

Getting across on branches of trees

The bicycle was another possibility, which suffered from two disadvantages. You could carry practically no luggage, which meant sleeping on the kangs in Chinese inns, and you lost "face" when you turned up to visit a territory manager on a push-bike. In exasperation at the funereal pace of travel, I acquired a motor-bike, hoping to ride it on the tracks next to the permanent way on the railways. This worked quite well, until you came to a railway bridge, from which the steel plating beneath the sleepers had been removed, to reveal the swirling waters below. It also involved travelling light. With forms of conveyance other than bicycle, motor-bike or wheelbarrow, my "No. 1 boy" usually came with me, as cook and general factotum.

In Taiyuan, the capital of the neighbouring province of Shanxi, the company had a Ford car, but its radius of action was small. Motor cars had a rough passage, as only one or two roads had a tarmac surface, without which they were either deep in mud or dust, according to the time of year. The narrow, metal-shod wheels of the carts bit deep into the surface, unless there was some sort of stone bottoming. There were a few miserable bus services: private individuals hardly dared own a motor-car, for fear of its confiscation by the military. Storms frequently washed away whole sections of the roads, the gaps being temporarily made good by the branches of trees.

The author with the staff of a territorial office

It was time to make the first sortie, and visit one of the territory managers, and I chose Baoding, one of the biggest cities in the division. It was the provincial capital of Hebei province. During the Boxer rising in 1900, a number of Christian missionaries had been murdered there, and the newly laid tracks of the Peking-Hankow Railway torn up.

It was some time since the last visit by a foreigner to the territory office. After a physical check of the stocks, and an examination of the books, a photograph was taken of all the staff with me in the middle, and I was told that the next day there would be a feast, at which I would be the guest of honour; one or two of the local dealers had been asked, and some senior members of the staff would be present.

Food looms large in the Chinese way of life, and an invitation to be the chief guest at a feast implies that you are respected, and means that you are being "given face". Protocol demands a round table; the host, sitting next to the chief guest, who faces the entrance to the room, has a special pair of chopsticks, with which he regales him with the choicest tit-bits from the mounting number of dishes on the table. There are "great dishes" and "small dishes", according to their size and importance. The menu for a dinner might be as follows: first the cold appetisers—duck fritters, octopus feelers, squares of fish and slivers of liver, with celery and peppers. The main dish—A great baked mandarin fish, followed by roast pork and a whole chicken, with meat balls and hearts of cabbage. Then a steamed pudding of sticky rice, with nuts, raisins, greengages, pineapple and laichees. To conclude—a small portion of rice, with boiling hot meat broth, accompanied by platefuls of shredded raw vegetables. Tea is provided throughout the meal, with possibly a warm yellow wine, a grape wine or, in North China, a spirit known as "pai ke", which is not unlike Irish poteen. No feast is complete without an airtight tin of 50 Three Castles cigarettes (San Pao Tai), regarded as the most luxurious brand of Virginia cigarette obtainable.

It is desirable that the foreign guest be well plied with drink, and to this end the "scissors-stone-paper" game is then played. Two people each shoot out their right hand, with either two fingers out (scissors), no fingers out (stone), or all five fingers out (paper). Scissors cut paper, paper wraps up stone and stone blunts scissors. The odds against the foreigner are heavy: the loser has to drink his small glass of wine or spirits, turn his glass upside down, and shout "Gan Bei" or "dry glass", to prove that he has done it. In another more sophisticated version of the game, the two contestants shoot out any number of fingers of the right hand, or none at all, at the same time, each shouting out what he believes to be the total number of fingers shown by both. This is an even worse bet from the foreigner's point of view: the Chinese are remarkably quick witted, and deft of finger.

Chinese food needs a whole volume to itself. Every province has its own specialities, the Cantonese being noted for bizarre sea food dishes, such as dried jelly fish and sea slugs; also snakes and bears' paws.

The sale of cigarettes was nearly all in single pieces for a small number of copper cash, a circular coin with a hole in the middle, which could be strung like beads on a string. Before the introduction of a paper currency, trade was transacted in the silver dollar and the copper cash, the values of which in terms of each other fluctuated according to ruling world prices. It was important, therefore, that single cigarettes should be available for an exact number of copper cash, which would allow a sufficient margin of profit to the dealers: wide fluctuations in the price of silver or copper caused a change in the demand for different brands. The copper/silver dollar exchange rate was a key factor in the promotion of different brands of cigarettes.

From time to time, arising out of some incident in a treaty port, or the death of a Chinese at the hands of a foreigner, boycotts of foreign goods were staged, which were highly effective, and endangered the trade in BAT cigarettes. Their remedy was to push the sale of brands belonging to a Chinese subsidiary.

The Chinese are not without patience and resourcefulness in matters commercial. The extraction for sale of single cigarettes from 10s or 20s packets left empties lying about, and it was not unknown for hand-made imitations of the machine made product, complete with the name of the brand on the cigarette itself, to be sold as the genuine article: purchasers seldom returned a second time!

The company had just started simple poster advertising on the railways and such roads as there were. They also ran a so-called "carton redemption scheme": the 10s and 20s packets were packed in stiff cardboard cartons, on the return of which to the dealers a small premium was paid. When sufficient cartons had been collected, they were burnt under supervision, to prevent their being used a second time. Occasionally there would be damage by water or pilferage, which were the subject of insurance claims.

Every month I had to send into the company a report on conditions in the country, as well as one on trade and competition. The following are some extracts from these reports, which throw some light on conditions in China's interior. *April 1931*. Riding the motor-bike alongside the railway tracks is less of a joy than I expected, owing to the absence of steel plates below the sleepers on the bridges. However, I made a triumphal entry into Baoding, where the police and military, overawed by the machine, forgot to ask for my passport. *May 1931*. Having taken five hours to go 30 miles through the cornfields, I decided that wisdom was the better part of valour, left the motor-bike at Xingjiawan and completed the journey on a gent's cycle. *May 1931*. Our office at Shuntehfu has been virtually commandeered by 20 soldiers who make such a din, that concentration on one's work is impossible. The Xunde region is, at the moment, quite unsuited to anything but the most fleeting of visits. Outside my door in the mornings, six or seven soldiers are wielding gigantic swords, which must date back to some very early dynasty: as they brandish the swords above their heads, they shout in unison, "Yi, er, san, si"—"one, two, three, four", the emphasis being on "si", then bring the sword down as if decapitating a victim, at the same time shouting "sha" or "kill", the whole performance being accompanied by horrible grimaces and sucking noises. (Decapitation was, of course, the normal method of executing criminals, though shooting is now more common). *May 1931*. I have just returned from Daming, which is just in Hebei province, but distant only 12 miles from

The depot staff

Shandong in the east, and the same distance from Henan in the south—what the Germans would call a "Knotenpunkt". Its close proximity to the provincial boundaries has given it the unenviable reputation of harbouring bandits, robbers, secret societies and bandit insurance concerns. There follows an undated telegram, reading, "Express never started last night: if it fails again, coming slow train tomorrow."* There follows an extract from an expenses statement. "Hire of mule—Yizhou to Lingqiu— $60.00 for nine days: cart hire, plus tip—$4.50." *June 1931.* The trip to Lingqiu is a very arduous one, but the mountain scenery beautiful. I went by mule litter. I got back to Chozhou yesterday on a bicycle from Yizhou, the first wheeled conveyance I had seen for many days. The Peking-Hankow Express is behaving in the most erratic manner: Major Page, who arrived from Peking yesterday, said he was a mere twenty-four hours late. *August 1931.* On a journey by boat to Shenjai, I noticed ahead of us two or three boats, tied up at the water's edge, the occupants of which appeared to be stepping out on to the bank, where they were obviously being searched by armed men, others of whom were searching the boats, while their occupants were on shore. An armed hold-up in fact. My territory manager was shaking

---

Owing to the absence of phonetics in the language, telegrams between two Chinese who knew no English, present a problem. The sender's ideographs are code numbered, and then decoded back to ideographs at the recipient's post office.

Two boats

with fear, and far too frightened to do anything but cower down below deck: I, too, was frightened (we had no weapons), but felt it was too great an indignity to go and join the queue. Bluff has always been a strong characteristic of the Chinese: if successful, it is better than confrontation. I decided to mount the 16 mm Bell and Howell cine camera on its tripod on the deck, put on dark sun glasses, and crouch menacingly behind it, as we passed the robbers. It worked like a charm—they made no move to stop us.*[1] *September 1931.* Xunde has been the scene of some pretty bad fighting and ghastly outrages. *September 1931.* In view of the present situation and general unrest, it seems inadvisable to go roaring through Shanxi with an open exhaust, so I am leaving the motor-bike at Datong (at which place it was subsequently sold to the son of a warlord). *November 1931.* Reports from our district manager at Suidezhou (in Shaanxi province, west of the Yellow River) are not re-assuring. It seems unwise to leave the province of Shanxi, though the much advertised bubonic plague in that province does not appear to be spreading. *November 1931.* Shanxi province has seldom been in a more disturbed state. There have been frequent cases of

*[1]*It was commonplace in China at this time for bandits and robbers to get busy as soon as the kaoliang is ripe—kaoliang is a kind of sorghum crop, which grows to seven or eight feet high. There was, in fact a field of it growing close to the river's edge.*

Time off for golf

banditry on the main roads, while the annexation of Manchuria by the Japanese in September has led to a serious shortage of funds.*² There follows an extract from the October edition of the *Shanxi Daily News*. "There is a very serious plague raging in West Shanxi and North Shaanxi this year. The people are getting frightened, and are scattering in all directions. In four xian alone, 3,000 people have died. Dr. Wan (undoubtedly the American Dr. Watson mentioned elsewhere), from the mission station, has ordered the provincial government to suspend the ferry services across the Yellow River, to prevent the spread of the infection into his area." *November 1931.* Letter from Mrs. P.T. Watson, wife of Dr. Watson at the Fenzhou hospital and mission station: "Dr. Watson has been away for two weeks trying to stop the epidemic of bubonic and pneumonic plague in the Linxian district. It is the most serious they have had, with over 200 villages affected. We appreciate very much your offer of help, and we may later call on you. We can give you inoculation against bubonic plague here in the hospital: there is no protection against pneumonic plague". *February 1932.* I safely delivered 115,000 dollars in silver to the Hongkong and Shanghai Bank in Peking, having accompanied the consignment on the slow train from Baoding. *Later.* The funds, totalling 150,000 dollars, came today by motor-car from Hejian. I hope that some other

*² *Shanxi has always been well-known for its banking activities.*

Yellow River

means of remitting funds will soon be found, as the transport of small fortunes in derelict motor-cars seems dangerous in the extreme.

Of the two and a half years I was in the Luhan division, one year was spent in Shanxi province, based on the capital, Taiyuan.

Access to the province was by rail from Shijiazhuang. A much more roundabout approach by rail from Peking was via Datong, the biggest town in North Shanxi, on the Peking-Suiyuan railway.

Taiyuan office

Imagine the delight of our small foreign community, when my firm decided to build a nine-hole golf course for a local general called **Zhang Zhen**, who was very westernised in his outlook, wore western style clothes, and had made the acquaintance of golf in one of the treaty ports. They went even further, and sent up one of their men from Shanghai, to give him instruction in the game. He turned out immaculately dressed in white shorts and stockings, but usually had at least one air shot off the tee.

The quid pro quo for the golf course was some relaxation in the mounting taxation of our product in the province. Revenue is the chief attraction of cigarettes to governments the world over, and China was certainly no exception to the rule.

Before the expiry of my four-year contract, I was determined to see the Yellow River, China's sorrow, which for centuries had claimed the lives of so many millions, when it flooded the plains of North China. It rises in Tibet, not far from China's other great river, the Yangtse, flows east, makes a sharp turn to the south, and then later another sharp turn to the east, before crossing the North China plain, and entering the Yellow Sea. The north-south section of its course is the boundary between the provinces of Shanxi and Shaanxi. My firm had a small depot at Suidezhou, on the West side of the river; the object of the visit was to discover whether any additional taxes were being levied in Shaanxi province.

Leaving Taiyuan in the office car, with the chauffeur, a man from the district office, and my No. 1 boy, we made for Fenzhou, about 70 miles southwest. The dirt road, its surface cut up by cars travelling on it immediately after heavy rain, enabled one to average about 20 mph with luck, and after about three hours, we could see the crenellated walls of the city standing out against the skyline. They were still intact: many city walls have been the targets of artillery fire in the civil wars, which seldom penetrates them, but frequently cuts off the crenellations.

Twisting in and out through various gates, we eventually entered the city, its narrow streets cart-rutted and pot-holed, incredibly dirty, and crowded with peasants and wonks (the native dogs). Dense clouds of dust rose behind any cart, rickshaw, or bicycle which moved.

The car was unloaded at our district office, and I visited the Yamen (more or less the equivalent of the municipal buildings) to enquire about the road to Liulin, our Shanxi destination. The magistrate was out: his assistant, a native of Yunnan province, who had been in Shanxi for 20 years, had never heard of the place: I presented my passport, an enormous folded sheet of rice paper covered with Chinese characters, to him; his scrutiny suggested that he was unable to read most of it. The Post Office was the next port of call, as I had a letter of introduction to the postmaster from the Danish inspector in Taiyuan. He hummed and hawed, said there were bandits on the road, but believed them "not to be dangerous". "You would be well advised to proceed slowly and with circumspection," he said, mournfully.

Then to the American mission hospital run by Dr. Watson, a Scotsman by birth, who came from Minnesota, had spent 23 years in the town, and had built up a magnificent, modern hospital. It was now overrun by soldiery, who had no money to pay their bills. He spoke of last year's plague in the district, communicated to human beings by fleas off rats, and at the moment dormant, the end of June being the earliest date on which he had known a recrudescence of the disease. "You might be well advised to have a plague injection, but one is hardly sufficient, and the second could not be made until a fortnight later."

May 30th is the anniversary of the day in 1925, when a number of Chinese students were killed by foreign police during a riotous procession in the International Settlement in Shanghai, an anniversary which was subsequently used to stir up anti-Imperialist feeling. As I came out of the hospital, I met a body of Feng Yu Xiang's men marching along the street, with propaganda flags stuck in the muzzles of their rifles instead of bayonets. Flags were out, and there were parades of students.

Dr. Watson told me he had been visited the previous evening by a man beating a gong, who threatened to fine him a dollar, if he didn't attend the Communist meeting on the following day. Two thousand of Feng Yu Xiang's officer students were said to be living in the town, which contained all the familiar seeds of another civil war.

The next morning two farm carts and two armed guards, sent by the magistrate, were waiting outside our dealer's shop at 6 am, and we eventually got off at 6.45. The Chinese are nothing if not early risers.

In 1921, at a time of dire famine distress, the American Red Cross had built a road going west to Liulin, at a cost of 250,000 dollars. The narrow, metal-shod wheels of carts had long since effectively ruined its surface, and it had become impassable for motor vehicles. Made of tamped earth, it was 25 feet across, the bridges being of stone or brick and mortar. Appalling dust lay at least a foot deep in the ruts, and we made about three miles an hour, to reach a small inn about midday. The well water was the colour of mud, and flies were in myriads.

The stop here lasted an hour and a half, as they said the mules would have to climb, and must have a full stomach: the feed consisted almost entirely of chopped straw. Nothing disturbed the monotonously slow tempo, to which one had to become accustomed, always ready to resume a more normal tempo, if the need arose.

The inn was at about 3,000 feet, and at last we rumbled on again, still rising. The thick loess soil, built up of dust blown for centuries off the Gobi desert, now started to give way to a rock formation, and the road had been blasted out at some points. Intermittent showers cooled the air and partially laid the suffocating dust. There was plenty of game to be seen, with chicor chuckling on the slopes of the hills, some pigeons and an occasional pheasant; it was ideal country to harbour game, with scrubby hills, broken by patches of cultivation. Wild pig were also reported in the district.

After about twenty two miles we reached our stopping place at Wangchi, a small village at 3,750 feet, boasting an inn, and a "garrison" of about 20 men. The guard commander, an ex-Shanxi soldier, had a broken finger on his right hand, and had been burnt and shot out of his hiding place in the hills by the bandits, while spying on their activities. He kept contradicting himself in his statements, tried to telephone to Fenzhou to report the arrival of the foreigner, but quickly dropped the instrument, when he remembered there had just been a thunderstorm, which apparently rendered it useless for the rest of the day. He said a Frenchman, armed to the teeth, and accompanied by six armed bodyguards, had passed the previous day, but he knew neither his name, nor his destination.

Off again the next morning punctually at 6 am with a body-guard of nine men, eight with rifles and one with a noisy, but ineffective, Browning automatic. The commander said a body of armed robbers had been reported in a neighbouring village the previous night, but that there was no danger. As we started climbing up a winding road, blasted out of the mountainside, one of the guards said, "We routed 90 bandits over there on the other side of the valley last year, and it was just here that the bandits killed a man from Henan, for giving away their secrets".

The top of the hill was about five miles from our starting point. Three roe deer moved across the opposite slope, while the hillsides were literally sizzling with pheasants: a sports-man's paradise, in fact, were it not for the bandits. Four xian boundaries met at the summit, each with its own defence organisation, which no doubt largely accounted for the bandit activity. Down from the summit to Wucheng, some 13 miles from our starting point, where we had lunch.

From here to Lishixian, the next stopping point, both sides of the valley were terraced and cultivated, with loess soil as far as the eye could see. We were still being escorted, a privilege handsomely paid for. At one place all the soldiers were away chasing the bandits, who had gutted a village on the previous night. Two individuals came forward, however, one with a prehistoric rifle, and the other with a couple of stick bombs. Enquiries about the situation elicited that "there had been some 'small affairs' down the road," which presumably referred to the looting of an entire village the night before. It is strange how major confrontations are written down in the Far East; after their invasion of China proper in July 1937, the Japanese always referred to hostilities as "the China affair", never to the "China War": perhaps the former description leaves the door more open to negotiation.

At Lishixian, there was a pretentious two-storeyed inn, where the gossip was all about bandits and opium smuggling, which seemed to be causing all the trouble. Officially it was a government monopoly, priced at two dollars an ounce, making it quite a profitable venture for smugglers in an inadequately policed area.

It was very dry, with little humidity in the air: appropriately, as the sun went down, a temple gong boomed out from a small rain temple across the valley. Shanxi province has, for centuries, been cursed by recurring droughts and famines.

The next day was searingly hot in this countryside of brown hills: one began to realise that the lives of millions of Chinese depended on a single fall of rain. As we plodded on, a considerable equipage in mule litters and on donkeys came past, which looked like some official returning home with his wife and family. The gentleman had that wizened look and yellow skin, which are the marks of the opium addict. On the left, a man clinging precariously to the hillside, was working a wooden plough pulled by a bullock. Bandits were reported scarce, and we had no guards at this point.

Liulin, after 20 miles of rough going, was in a pleasant location and blessed with running water—almost like an oasis in the desert—and we spent the day here. I had a German wirehaired retriever with me, and bathed with him: the locals referred to him as a "grrrr", apparently the code-name for all the species.

The road to our original destination, Suidezhou in Shaanxi, was reported clear by the postman, but our dealer had a letter from his agent, stating it was completely unsafe. It turned out that there were two roads, one safe and the other dangerous, the latter being used by those with baggage, as one would expect. We decided to give Suidezhou a miss.

I visited a temple in the old walled city, in which was a large bronze Buddha, which the inhabitants were trying to sell, to raise money to build a school. This seemed to be a common practice all over North China, and probably accounted for the large number of Buddhas on sale in the curio shops.

We set off at 7.30 the next morning for the Yellow River, the road leading along a well watered valley for about six miles, then ascending sharply for three miles, to drop another three down to the deep gorge through which the river flowed. The loess, about 500 feet thick, had a weird effect on the traveller, who saw a sea of brown devoid of human habitation. Suddenly a shower of dirt fell on my head, indicating a flock of goats high up above; on the road there was an occasional pedlar, or a man on a donkey. There was a parching, dry wind. No wonder crops failed under these conditions: there was a terrible drought here during the great famine of 1921.

Suddenly we came on the small stone village of Chundu, perched about a hundred feet above the swirling, eddying, mud brown water of the river, which rustled and curled itself up into odd-shaped waves on its downward course. The banks on both sides must be over 200 feet high, the far one in Shaanxi province looking like the edge of a godless desert.

Below the village, two ferry boats were waiting—square ended, wooden craft, about 25 feet long, with an eight foot beam. A man was busy patching up a hole in the bottom of our boat with cottonwool. The holes were numerous, and there must have been a good two inches of water in the bottom of the boat. Forty persons, five mules, and a mule litter came on board, the last-named prodded by a soldier with a loaded revolver. I unlaced my boots, as a fly, stinging the mules in their rumps, could easily have made them drive their hooves through the floorboards. The boatmen, all strong swimmers, seemed quite unconcerned.

As we moved off, two individuals on each side started manipulating the clumsy 12-foot oars used to negotiate the boat through the swiftest part of the current, where it rocked and swayed, to the accompaniment of fearful yells from the boatmen. We had gone about half a mile downstream on reaching the far bank of the river, which is only about 200 yards across at this point.

Songjiachuan, the village on the Shaanxi side, boasted a tax office, which I had come to visit, a motley collection of very rude soldiery, two or three policemen and an inn. Shaanxi, renowned for its bandits and opium, was living up to its reputation, for about three acres of the beautifully shaped, white opium poppies, spaced about a foot apart, were immediately apparent on landing. The harvesting of the crop, after the flowers have faded, is apparently the work of specialists, who slice open the pods, and extract the maximum amount of juice from them.

Some nine exhausted-looking gentlemen were seated in the tax office, a two-storeyed, fly-blown shack, where imposts were being levied on all and sundry, according to their ability to pay. I was given a "Book of the Rules", purchased sufficient tax stamps for the two small cases of cigarettes we had brought, and hurried away from the place. We had come a long way to establish the rate of tax being levied, which, in the central government's eyes, was illegal, but it was very doubtful if anything could, or would, be done about it: the writ of the central government carried little weight in these parts.

The boatmen had hauled the ferries upstream for the return trip, and by evening we were back in Chundu village on the Shansi bank. As twilight fell, the walls of Wupu, on the Shaanxi side, were clearly silhouetted against the Western sky: a temple gong boomed out thrice: the local defence force sang its war songs, and I went to sleep, lulled by the lapping of the Yellow River waters—an unforgettable experience.

This was the last long trip I made in the interior in pre-revolutionary China, as the time for returning home on leave was approaching, and I had decided not take on another contract—a wise decision in the light of subsequent events in the Far East.

Before the days of long distance air travel, the Trans Siberian railway, advertised in those days as "Peking to Paris in ten days", was the quickest way of returning to Europe. The journey was not without incident, as Manchuria was in the hands of the Japanese, and we had a wait of two days at Manchuli, the border town between Manchuria and Russia, for some unspecified reason. The Japanese were certainly throwing their weight about, and not letting you forget that they were masters of the country.

The locomotives on the Siberian railway, which was then single-tracked, burnt wood, usually completed the journey on time. There were two classes, second and third, the latter with wooden seats on both sides of a gangway, and obviously most uncomfortable. On enquiring why there were two classes of passenger in this utopian, egalitarian state, I was told that "things were still in a state of transition!" I suppose they still are.

IV
1932—1974

ABSENCE is said to make the heart grow fonder: mine was one of 42 years before revisiting China in 1974. Later chapters will tell whether the heart has grown fonder or not.

But first let me highlight some of the most important events which happened during these 42 years, the first 17 of which were almost entirely devoted either to war with Japan, or to civil war between Chiang K'ai-shek and Mao Ze Dong, and the last 25 to the establishment of Communism. During the whole of this period I was completely out of touch with China, apart from one amusing incident during the war against Germany in Europe.

I had the misfortune to be captured by the Germans near St. Valery-en-Caux, while serving with the Fifty First Highland Division in France in June 1940. In the summer of 1941 my wife suddenly got an urgent message from the then War Office, addressed to me, which read, "Understand you are fluent speaker of Mandarin Chinese; report next Tuesday to Dept. C.O. for special duties". It did so happen that I had five brief days of liberty, running about in Germany at about this time, having escaped from a prison camp, but it was a pretty long shot on the part of the War Office.

War and Civil War, 1932–1949. The Japanese had invaded Manchuria in 1931, and had soon after renamed it "Manchukuo", having installed, as Emperor of their new creation, Pu Yi, the unfortunate Emperor elect of China at the time of the Revolution there in 1911. In pursuit of their aim of creating a "Greater Asia", of which they were to be masters, they were busy infiltrating North China, by trying to unify its currency with that of Manchukuo, by suborning as many Chinese as possible, by encouraging smuggling, partly in aid of their exports and partly to deprive the Chinese government of Customs revenue, and by creating an opium monopoly in Manchukuo and the adjoining province of Re He, which steered a high proportion of its products into China proper. This monopoly was described by the advisory committee of the League of Nations as "the biggest single venture ever undertaken in the illicit traffic in narcotics".

Initially there was a civil governor of Manchuria, but, with the advent of the new state, he was replaced by a soldier. In the samurai tradition, the Japanese have a long history of militarism; in recent years, when the military ousted the civilians, wise counsels seldom prevailed. The military were intent on the subjugation of China, come what may.

On July 7th, 1937, there was an armed clash between Chinese and Japanese soldiers at Lukouqiao, just outside Peking, and better known to foreigners as the Marco Polo Bridge. Each side blamed the other for starting the fight; to the Chinese it became known as the "Double Seventh"—they have an ingrained habit of commemorating dates in this way, particularly in cases where they have suffered defeat or ignominy. The Japanese referred to this and the subsequent war as the "China Incident" or the "China Affair".

The incident did indeed lead to a spread of the war, which developed in three phases. On August 13th, the Japanese attacked Shanghai and, having taken it, captured Nanking in December, where an orgy of murder, looting and rape took place. This phase saw the only large-scale pitched battle between Chiang K'ai-shek's forces and the Japanese, when the Chinese held up a strong force making its way South from Peking, at a place called Taierzhuang. The second phase led to the capture of Hankow and Canton in October 1938, and in the final stage the Chinese Central Government moved to Chongqing, on the upper reaches of the Yangtse river, where it remained until the end of the Second World War. Apart from a resurgence of Japanese activity in 1944, mainly directed against airports being used by American aircraft, the war in China was virtually a stalemate, exept for guerrilla activities, mainly carried out by the communists operating from Yanan. Many thousands of Japanese troops, of course, who could be ill spared, were tied down on garrison duties.

In the political sphere, great efforts were made by the Japanese to set up a Chinese government hostile to Chiang K'ai-shek, notably that of Wang Jing Wei, a defector from the Chongqing government. He died in Japan in 1944, and could be described as the Quisling of the Far East.

One effect of the Japanese invasion of the mainland was to drive tens of thousands of Chinese, and some industries, into the west and Southwest of the country, which came to be known as "Free China". This involved greater food production and the setting up of war industries.

Then, on December 7th, 1941, came the Japanese attack on Pearl Harbour in all its suddenness, to be followed by the fall of Singapore and the rapid advance of the Japanese up into Burma, from where China had been receiving most of her supplies over the Burma road. The closure of this avenue meant that she was cut off entirely from the outside world, except for the overland route from the hard pressed Soviet Union. All the supplies sent by the Western powers and the Soviet Union went to Chongqing. The Communists fended for themselves and relied on captured weapons, and such crude weapons as they could make for themselves. Not until the air route from India, "over the hump" as it was called, was opened, were supplies resumed from the West: by January 1945, 44,000 tons a month were being flown in.

Inside China, the Red Army in Jiangxi province had successfully resisted no less than five major offensives to encircle it, before embarking on the hazardous Long March in late 1934. Mao set up his new headquarters at Yanan in Shaanxi province in 1935, from where he administered the sparsely populated northwest border region, which was to prove a valuable experimental area for all the measures he intended to carry out when leader of the whole country. As Chiang K'ai-shek's regime, virtually a military dictatorship and police state, grew more unpopular, so did Mao's strength increase, in numbers and influence. His Eighth Route Army was seen to be the only force offering real resistance to the Japanese invaders: in a major battle at Pingxingguan, the Japanese suffered 3,000 casualties: this was the only major battle fought between the Japanese and the Communists, who relied later more on guerrilla tactics and harassment of the enemy.

The seventh plaque on the Memorial to the Heroes of the Revolution in Peking depicts the active resistance to the Japanese invaders.

The Americans, who had consistently supported Chiang K'ai-shek, and had supplied large quantities of arms to him, began to realise the dangers of a power struggle and civil war in China, well before the end of the Second World War, and did their best to bring the two sides together. General Marshall, sent over to effect a reconciliation between Chiang and Mao, did succeed in arranging a truce and cease-fire for a time, but a full scale civil war erupted in 1947, leading to Mao's final victory in 1949. His earliest successes were in Russian-occupied Manchuria, which led to the conclusion that there was collusion between the Red Army and the Soviet Union: this was not borne out by facts, as not a single Russian weapon was to be seen at the victory parade held in Peking.

The Americans, well posted about the strength and discipline of the Red Army by their consular representatives, had backed the wrong horse. Fuel was added to the fire by the help they gave Chiang K'ai-shek to establish his regime on the island of Taiwan, previously Japanese occupied Formosa.

HMS Amethyst

In 1941 the Russians had signed a Neutrality Pact with the Japanese, which they abrogated two days after the first atomic bomb fell on Hiroshima. They overran the whole of Manchuria in three weeks, the future of which was settled for the time being by a Sino-Russian Treaty of Alliance and Friendship.

The sun finally set on Imperialist power and influence in China with the epic escape of the British frigate *Amethyst* from under the noses of the Communists on the Yangtse River near Nanking in April 1949. In just over the span of a man's lifetime, reckoning from the conclusion of the Opium War in 1840, foreign influence had reached its peak in the early 20th century, and then slowly ebbed away.

The eighth plaque on the Memorial to the Heroes of the Revolution in Peking depicts Mao's troops crossing the Yangtse to capture Nanking in April 1949.

The 17 years from 1932–1949 brought great suffering to the Chinese people and the loss of millions of lives. For much of the time the country was divided into three parts—occupied China, garrisoned by the Japanese and their puppets in the main centres and always subject to guerrilla attacks, if they ventured out of them—'Free China', again divided into the main part controlled by Chiang and the Kuomintang from Chongqing, and the northwest border region, controlled by Mao from Yanan.

The situation for foreigners had been deteriorating for many years, particularly since 1927, with the upsurge of the Kuomintang, the rise of Chinese nationalism, and the wave of anti-imperialist feeling. For foreign business men the intrusion of Japan brought many trade restrictions: after the Japanese took Shanghai in 1937, the Yangtse river was virtually closed to all traffic. Pearl Harbour dealt the final blow, and brought the complete cessation of all foreign trade, except Japanese. This is an account by a resident of what happened in Shanghai at the time of Pearl Harbour and thereafter.

"On Sunday, December 6th, 1941, life in Shanghai was going on in the normal way, as at any ordinary week-end in peacetime. Race courses, clubs, hotels and restaurants were functioning as usual and people went to bed on Sunday night with no ideas other than that the normal week would commence the next morning, 7th December.

"The first intimation of anything untoward in Shanghai took place in the small British gunboat moored in the Huangpu River, the only British naval vessel moored in the port. The Japanese Admiral at Shanghai sent a boarding party to the ship calling on its commander to surrender; on his refusal, a Japanese cruiser opened fire and practically blew the ship out of the water. Any survivors trying to swim ashore were then fired on, and those not killed were captured and imprisoned until the end of the war. While this was going on, most people in Shanghai were still asleep in their homes. My own first news of the events was a telephone call from the duty officer at my office, telling me of Pearl Harbour, that the Japanese had taken control of the International Settlement in Shanghai, and advising me to stay in my house, and listen to the radio for further news.

"In due course instructions were broadcast by the Japanese authorities to the effect that all British and American residents in Shanghai were to report to Japanese Military Headquarters, to give up their cars and any arms they possessed, and to register with the Japanese authorities. Failure to do so would lead to unpleasant consequences.

"On registration, people were issued with passes, which had always to be shown to Japanese soldiers or officials, on demand. In due course the Japanese took control of all British and American concerns. The method was for Japanese commercial interests, under the control of the military, to liquidate the banks, shipping companies etc., in which process we were obliged to assist.

"As there were no cars, and as British and other foreign residents in Shanghai lived in most cases in residential areas far away from their offices, they were obliged to travel to their offices in trams and buses, a very crowded and uncomfortable form of transport in Shanghai at any time. Or else, as most of them eventually did, by bicycle, a matter of seven miles or so every day. This life continued throughout the very cold winter of 1941/42 and the very hot summer of 1942, with creature comforts like fuel, electricity, food, and drink especially, reduced to a minimum. All bank accounts had been liquidated by the Japanese and, when cash had run out, the only resources available were payments made through the Swiss consulate of £10 per head per month as a result of an agreement between the British and American governments and the Swiss government. These resources were supplemented unofficially through friendly Chinese commercial travellers. In all this the Chinese population were most helpful.

"During this time, the Japanese Secret Service Police imprisoned, and, in some cases, tortured and ill-treated a number of leading members of the community and other residents, whom they unjustly accused of having engaged in activities hostile to them. These included heads of British and American firms, presidents of international societies, such as, for example, the St. Andrew's Society, journalists, broadcasters and others. The method used was to send a squad of soldiers to the person's house at about 4 am, pull him out of bed, take him off to a prison containing all sorts of prisoners, criminals and convicts, and leave him there in the most disgusting sanitary conditions between painful interrogations and on starvation diet for an indefinite period. Many people suffered permanent defects from this treatment and some died from it."

A friend of mine and his companion managed to get out of Shanghai, before being caught up by the Japanese: this is how they got out.

"Their Chinese contact placed R. and Sidney, packed like two sardines, head to tail, in the boot of a small car, then drove to a nightclub to pick up a Japanese colonel, who had been bribed to get a load of contraband furs out of the city. At the nightclub, Sidney, who spoke Japanese, was dismayed to hear the colonel ask to see the consignment of furs, but he was fortunately dissuaded by the Chinese driver. R. at this time, with his nose only inches away from the colonel's backside the other side of the seat, was only afraid he might cough or sneeze: would he have the courage not to cry out if the Japanese guards should open the boot and stick a bayonet in?

"With the colonel beside the driver, the car passed through all the check-points with only a bow and a hiss from the sentries. Once in open country the colonel got out, and after driving a few miles further, R. and Sidney were also released from their very cramped positions.

"Asked later as to what he, the driver, would have done had the Colonel insisted on opening the boot, he laconically replied: 'I should have shot him.'"'

Missionaries, whose number in China had been substantially reduced by the time of Pearl Harbour, also suffered considerably. Here is an account of what happened to a friend of mine, a Baptist missionary.

"My wife and I lived in Chengzi in the northwest of China, as missionaries of the Baptist Missionary Society from 1924 to 1951, and during the period of the Communist war in 1936. The Communists were driven on the long march to Yanan, and that is when we met many of them. We were living in Xian and, of course, travelled up north and they travelled down south. I met Zhou En Lai particularly, and I have a very great respect for him as the moderate, and the peacemaker, and the man of wisdom of the whole Party.

"During that time of fraternisation with the Communists, another incident happened, which was the Xian incident. Chiang K'ai-shek was captured in Xian, and for two weeks we did not know what was going to happen; ultimately he was released by the Communists, who negotiated the policy of the united front against the Japanese; during that time Zhou En Lai came down from Yanan and met the Chinese and foreign leaders of the church and made a deep impression on us all; a man with a price on his head, he had a brilliant intellect and fine character; he told us for the first time the new policy of the Communist Chinese government towards religion, namely that they would guarantee freedom of religious belief and worship, but not freedom to convert and preach.

"During that time also another incident happened, which concerned us personally. In 1941 we had a telegram from Shanghai, which read 'Your three children are prisoners of war in the hands of the Japanese.' We were stunned by this message, not knowing anything of what had happened, and only later did we discover that the Japanese had bombed Pearl Harbour, sunk part of the American Navy and war had been declared. The Japanese had landed at Qufu and taken the scholars, two hundred children, and put them in an internment camp at Wazhen in Shandong. That was a tremendous shock to us. We were free during the next four years, and our children, with others, were prisoners of war. They were treated fairly well; later on they were released after the war in 1945; we met them, and they settled down with us in Edinburgh."

Foreign individuals in other parts of China had many exciting adventures. Michael Lindsay, in his book, *The Unknown War 1937–1945* describes in great detail his escape from Peking, life in the Communist-held areas of North China and finally life in Chongqing.

The story of what happened to the few remaining foreigners when Mao took power in October 1st, 1949, has yet to be told. Some of those in Shanghai were compelled to stay on, to keep running their businesses and to pay handsomely for the privilege of doing so. Others, notably some Roman Catholic missionaries, were imprisoned, and subjected to thought reform for many months, under most unpleasant conditions.

Communist rule 1949–1974. After years of war, China was in a state of exhaustion, with disrupted communications, raging inflation and industrial backwardness. If Mao wanted to put China back on her feet again, there was really no alternative to soliciting the help of the Soviet Union, which, on the face of it, had the same ideology and a fairly advanced industrial base. He went to Moscow in 1949, the first time he had ever been out of China, and nine weeks later signed the "Thirty Year Treaty of Friendship, Alliance and Mutual Assistance", which, amongst other clauses, provided for a loan of US$300 million repayable in five years, and the return to China of Manchuria and its railways, Dairen and Port Arthur still to be used by the Russians.

The London *Times*, commenting on the Treaty in a leading article, said, "The precise meaning of the new agreements between the Soviet Union and China will appear only when they are illuminated by the future actions of the two parties. It would be wholly at variance with Russian diplomatic practice, if the published document told the whole story; almost certainly there are secret protocols, or understandings, the terms of which will only emerge, when the time comes to put them into force". It was generally thought that the loan was a comparatively paltry sum, having regard to the immense problems facing the new People's Republic and the size of loans granted to much smaller countries inside the Communist bloc. Many saw in the Treaty the confirmation of a vast Communist world, extending from the Elbe to the Pacific, the forerunner of global Communism.

Within months of the creation of the People's Republic in 1949, the Korean War had broken out in 1950, when North Korea invaded the South and, after initial successes, was driven back by United Nations troops, right up to the Yalu River, the frontier between Manchuria and North Korea. The Chinese, always jealous of their frontiers, saw in this the advent of an American invasion, intervened with strong forces, described as "volunteers", and pushed back the United Nations troops, until held up by superior fire-power.

It is believed by many that the initiative for the war came from Stalin, who wanted to embroil and embarrass both the Chinese and the USA. Apart from Korea, these were the two powers which suffered the bulk of the casualties, while China additionally had to pay for most of the weapons she used, which came from the Soviet Union and were purchased on credit.

Anti-American feeling was at its height during the Korean war: thousands of mass meetings were held all over the country to "Resist the USA and aid Korea". Anyone remotely considered to be a counter revolutionary was arrested: many were shot.

The new regime's first priority was land reform. Mao, himself of peasant stock, understood the agricultural problems of his country and the outlook of the peasantry.

Against the advice of Moscow, which wanted an industrial revolution, he persisted with the revolution of the peasantry, with the promise of redistribution of land and the removal of land, power and privileges from the landlord. The Agrarian Law of 1950 resulted in mass meetings in the villages all over the country, at which landlords, and sometimes rich peasants, were publicly paraded and accused of past misdeeds and exploitation, in some cases being put to death by the villagers on the spot. Before the land redistribution took place, two thirds of the agricultural workers owned little or no land at all.

In 1951 the peasants were asked to form mutual aid teams by sharing implements, and helping each other when necessary: this was followed, first by semi-socialist co-operatives in 1953, and by full co-operatives in 1955, under which system all the land was pooled, and they were paid according to work done. The final goal, creation of the People's Communes, was reached in 1958. What had been planned to take eighteen years to complete, had been achieved in nine. In the words of the Central Committee's resolution to create the communes, "A new unit of agricultural production has been created, of grandiose historical significance, fresh as the rising sun appearing on the vast horizon of East Asia." The communes were to look after all aspects of social life, to own all property, to exercise complete power in economic matters, to merge with the local administrative authorities, and to be the stepping stone towards the final goal of a pure communist state. This extreme form of centralisation, imposed on them with such suddenness, met with a good deal of resistance from the peasants, as a result of which the 24,000 giant communes envisaged, were increased to 70,000 of smaller size, with much more authority and initiative delegated to smaller units farther down the scale. The Western press at this time was full of stories about giant barracks and communal dining rooms being built, which probably emanated from the proposal to create the smaller number of giant communes.

In 1955 a beginning was made with the take-over of industry and business concerns operated by Chinese capital, foreign owned enterprises having been nationalised from the outset. Here the government was on much less firm ground and proceeded with caution, such capitalists and entrepreneurs as there were being treated with much greater leniency than the landlords: many of them, in fact, were allowed to continue managing their concerns and were paid a small rate of interest on their invested capital.

The Russian loan of $300 million, arranged in 1950, was followed by two further loans totalling $750 million in 1955 and 1956, transactions thereafter being on a strictly cash basis. These Russian loans were used partly to restore communications, partly to assist with such prestige creations as the road and rail bridge over the Yangtse at Nanking, and partly to set up entirely new industries, of which the Chinese had had no experience. Large numbers of Russian technicians came into the country: Russian films were imported, as well as millions of translations of Lenin's works. Sino-Russian Friendship Societies sprang up in thousands. Russian became obligatory in the schools. It was rather a one sided honeymoon while it lasted.

In 1956 the denunciation of Stalin by Khruschev, at the 20th Congress of the Soviet Union's Communist party, caused a great stir and upheaval in the Communist world. Hopes of a less rigid application of Communist principles led to revolts in Poland and Hungary, which encouraged Mao to test the feelings and attitudes to the Communist Party of his own people. He did this by instituting the "Hundred Flowers" campaign— "let a hundred flowers bloom, let a hundred schools contend"— in which the people were encouraged to express their views and criticisms of the regime and the Party. Initial reaction was slow, but later developed into a storm of criticism. This was allowed to continue for five weeks, before the regime put a stop to it, and was followed by a "rectification" campaign directed at the "rightists", both inside and outside the Party.

In 1958, almost simultaneously with the creation of the People's Communes, the "Great Leap Forward" was started in a blaze of optimism, with fantastic statistics of the results to be expected from it. It was to be a massive national attempt to boost industrial production by every possible means, men being drafted into industry from the land, if necessary. Steel would be produced in home ovens by families after normal working hours. Prophecies were made of the date by which China would overtake the production of other industrialised countries: grossly exaggerated figures of the results being obtained were published. The "Leap", in fact, proved to be an utter failure, had repercussions on the following year's harvest, and greatly damaged the prestige of Mao himself.

As a result, Liu Shao Qi came to the fore as a possible contender for supreme power: he was a pragmatist, later to be labelled a "rightist", in direct contrast to Mao, the arch-revolutionary. In the early 1960s there were two bad harvests, which caused a good deal of under-nourishment, even starvation; this was followed by the sudden and complete withdrawal of all Russian technicians, who took with them plans of un-completed factories, and factory processes. Mao was content to lie low during this period of extreme difficulty; he had, in fact, relinquished his position as Head of State in 1958.

By 1964 he was again advocating a full resumption of the class struggle; his wife, Jiang Qing, started to purge the theatre and art circles of "rightists", insisting that literature and the theatre should serve the continuing revolution, and do away with traditional themes. Mao continually drove the Socialist Education Movement to create class consciousness in the communes, and further the cause of the poor peasants. The stage was being set for the last great act of his revolutionary career— the Great Proletarian Cultural Revolution, probably the biggest man-inspired upheaval the world has ever seen. No hint of this reached the outside world until July 1966, when Mao, then aged nearly 73, took to the waters of the Yangtse river before 200,000 spectators, and is said to have swum 15 kilometres downstream. This was followed by a mass distribution of millions of "Little Red Books" containing the "Thoughts of Mao", and lapel badges showing his face. The world at large could not comprehend what it was all about.

This was Mao's last move to ensure that the spirit of revolution, created by the sufferings of the Communist Party, was kept alive. He saw signs of flagging interest in the rising generation, and wanted to perpetuate the revolutionary spirit, for which he had striven so hard, the ultimate goal being the Utopian concept, that man should be rewarded according to his needs, and not according to the product of his work.

If foreigners found difficulty in understanding this new initiative of Mao, the Chinese people were left in little doubt. Thus the Peking *People's Daily*, "The Chinese people must rid themselves of the influence of all the traditions, and forces of habit of thousands of years, left over by the exploiting classes" and "The current sharp class struggle on the ideological and cultural front is one to shatter all schemes for capitalist restoration ideologically". The two main targets of attack were the teaching professions, and, later, members of the Communist

Party itself.

In old China, scholars and their teachers were held in high esteem. The following is an extract from the Li Chi, one of the standard books of Chinese classical literature in the seventh century A.D. "When a pupil meets his teacher on the road, he should hasten towards him and bow· If the teacher addresses him, he should give a suitable reply: if the teacher is silent, he should retire quickly. The pupil should wait upon his teacher, and should pay him the tribute of sincere mourning for three years after his death". And the following from a Communist Party directive at the outset of the Cultural Revolution. "Universities, middle schools and technical schools will be closed, in order that all students above primary school age can devote their time and energy to the Revolution. The first task of the students thus released from classes will be to attack their teachers, and charge them with being revisionists or persons, who secretly wish to return to the old ways and culture".

The attacks by wall posters, and in the press, were mild indeed in comparison with what followed. Teachers were beaten, tortured, forced to eat insects and excrement, hung up by their arms and legs, compelled to kneel on broken glass, and suffered other indignities· As Mao once said, "A revolution is not the same as inviting people to dinner, or writing an essay or painting a picture".

Students, and particularly those from the universities, soon became the spearhead of the Revolution. Those with impeccable proletarian backgrounds were entitled to become Red Guards and wear red arm-bands. A rally of over a million of them was held in the Tian An Men square in Peking in August, and was followed by several others. Here are two samples of their battle cries, "We are the Red Guards of Chairman Mao, and we effect the convulsion. We tear up and smash old calendars, precious vessels, U.S. and British records, superstitious lacquers, and ancient paintings, and we put up the picture of Chairman Mao". And again, "Old and young gentlemen of the landlord and bourgeois classes, we tell you frankly. You all stink and you are nothing special, just rotten trash. We detest you from our hearts! We hate you! We shall beat members of these exploiting classes, crunch them, smite them and their dog mouths, and our bayonets shall taste blood. We will smash the old world to smithereens, create a new world and carry the Great Proletarian Cultural Revolution through to the end."

"Bombard the Headquarters" was a slogan issued by Mao, as an incitement to the students to attack supposed "rightists" in the Communist hierarchy: the foreign ministry in particular was occupied by students for a fortnight. In October, revolutionary rebels in communes and factories were encouraged to "seize power from the power holders". It was thanks to the People's Liberation Army (the P.L.A.) that some sort of order was maintained: thanks to Zhou En Lai that the wheels of industry continued to turn, and the departments of government to function.

By 1969 the Revolution had begun to peter out, though some of the universities did not return to normal until the 1970s. Liu Shao Qi, who had aspired to supreme power, was first demoted to No. 8 in the hierarchy, and then expelled from the Communist Party in 1968. In 1971 Lin Biao, generally regarded as Mao's successor, perished mysteriously in an air accident with some of his supporters. A veteran of the Long March, he had much influence with the armed forces, whose power had grown considerably during the Cultural Revolution: he had been plotting Mao's overthrow, and paid the price for doing so.

In 1970 Mao's health began to fail: he died on September 6th, 1976, between my two visits in 1974 and 1977: the aftermath of his death is described in a later chapter. He had been chairman of the Politburo uninterruptedly for 41 years since his appointment in the early stages of the Long March at Zunyi in 1935. I did not see the vast memorial to him at the Tian An Men Square in Peking until a later visit in 1980.

V
Return to Peking, 1974

I WANTED to return to China, as I still speak good Mandarin, to make a film of it and possibly thereafter write a book. This was in 1973, when relatively few foreigners were being allowed into the country in the aftermath of the Great Proletarian Cultural Revolution, and before the entry of the travel agencies into the business. Not only that—I wanted to go alone, and not in a group.

I had the worst possible credentials, having served a four-year contract with a highly capitalist business in China, and having a political outlook which in no sense could be interpreted as left-wing. Six years' service in His Majesty's Forces in Hitler's war might be regarded as a plus: my trump card, however, was undoubtedly a good knowledge of the Mandarin tongue.

There could be no harm in trying out my Mandarin on the staff of the Chinese Embassy in Portland Place, London, I thought, so I went there several times, and made a friend of a member of the staff. After nine months I was eventually granted a visa for a visit of three weeks, to be organised by the China International Travel Service (CITS). A sensible provision in the visa allowed me to select any three consecutive weeks inside a six week period, which gave a welcome degree of flexibility, when making travel arrangements.

How to get there—to Peking, that is? There were three main routes from the United Kingdom. You could fly to Hongkong, and go by air or train to Peking from Canton, the train journey taking about two days and nights. You could fly direct to Peking from Heathrow by PIA, or from Orly Airport by Air France. It is no accident that these two countries fly there direct; Pakistan is politically a friend of China; France has always been a source of inspiration to the Chinese Communist Party, because of the French Revolution; after the First World War a number of Chinese students went there on work and study courses, including Zhou En Lai. Thirdly, you could go overland by train on the Trans Siberian Railway from Moscow to Peking, or indeed from East Berlin to Peking via Moscow, if you wanted to look at the main components of the communist world.

The Siberian route seemed much the most attractive and interesting to me. I had the Chinese visa, which was the most difficult to get, so I started off with some optimism to make enquiries about the other visas required for East Germany, Poland, the Soviet Union and Mongolia, aiming to go the whole way by train from East Berlin, and taking the Chinese train via Mongolia. Only transit visas were necessary for the first two, I was told: the Soviet Union might take some time: for Mongolia, a personal visit to their embassy was necessary. So off I posted to it at 7, Kensington Court, London, W.8., to be greeted by a charming Mongolian lady in European dress, to whom I explained the object of my visit. She produced two forms for completion, and asked for a fee of two pounds, which I handed over. On completion of the form, she asked, as if in an afterthought, whether I had a visa for the Soviet Union, to which I replied in the negative. "Ah! that's different" she said. "I can't give you a visa for Mongolia, until you produce one from the Soviet Union"—and pocketed the cash! "You'd better go to the Russian consulate in Bayswater Road." So off I posted there.

Right in the doorway of a rather large and shabby Victorian building stood an immobile London bobby, who paid scant attention to me, as I brushed past him into the entrance hall, where I was greeted by a short, stocky individual, looking like a prize-fighter. He asked my business, and then produced from his pocket what looked like a book of pink raffle tickets, from which he tore out No. 55, and handed it to me, then ushering me into an enormous reception room, in one corner of which sat a lonely male.

After about 10 minutes he re-appeared, beckoned me to follow him and showed me into a small office with two desks, manned by a young woman and a rather seedy looking clerk. I chose the latter, sat down, produced my passport with Chinese visa, indicated that I wanted to go to Peking on the Trans-Siberian Railway, and asked for a Soviet Union transit visa. "Have you booked your room in a Moscow hotel yet?" he said nonchalantly. "Not yet" I said, innocently. "Ah! That's different," he said triumphantly. "We cannot issue a transit visa until you have booked a room in a Moscow hotel."

The first contacts with communist bureaucracy were not very encouraging, and I saw visions of the necessary transit visas not materialising until after the expiry date on the Chinese visa. It was all very frustrating and led to a decision to take the easiest way out, and go by air. China and Pakistan were on good terms: it might create a good impression if I went on a Pakistani plane, so I opted for that.

Purchase of a tourist class ticket presented no problem; the photographic equipment weighed exactly 21 lb and the clothes the same. I had hoped to take a 16 mm. cine camera, but ever since an Italian film operator called Antonioni made a film, which the Chinese thought did them no credit, tourists have been restricted to 8 mm, which cannot be used for television work or national network.

The plane stopped briefly at Orly Airport and Frankfurt, and reached Islamabad in about seven hours: I had forgotten it is now the capital of Pakistan, and was in earlier days Rawalpindi, the most important military base in that part of undivided India. There was a three-hour stop and we were given a tour round the old military quarter of the city. Never have I seen so many old Morris cars on the streets: the old garrison church of St. Paul still seemed to be functioning, and there were many other signs of the old British rule in India.

Off again, unfortunately at a time which meant we should miss flying over the Himalayas in daylight. Quite a number of Chinese had now come aboard: they sat in groups, and looked as if they were government employees of some kind. Communism doesn't tolerate the individual, unless he is seen to belong to a group.

We took another nine hours to reach Peking. As I walked down the gangway in the dark with my two bags, I was surprised to see two young girls come rushing up to give me a hand with the baggage, an offer I gladly accepted. Inside the reception hall I produced my passport and baggage for examination by a customs man, who was obviously not keen on foreigners, though in no way openly hostile. Then from a darker corner of the hall two people loomed up, and asked if I was "Mr. Lo"—one a diminutive woman who introduced herself as "Mrs. Li", the other a sturdily built young man, who introduced himself as "Mr. Wang." Mrs. Li was apparently responsible for all the European visitors to the capital: Mr. Wang was an interpreter with the Chinese International Travel Service (CITS) and was to be my constant companion and adviser for the next three weeks.

Outside, a black saloon car was waiting, its side windows draped with those damask curtains, of which the Chinese are so fond. It was a journey of some 40 kilometres to the centre of Peking, down a tarmac avenue lined on both sides with trees. As I was to learn later, tree planting and afforestation have played a big part in planning since Liberation in 1949: I specifically mention "Liberation", and not "revolution", as the Chinese see the new order as having swept away every vestige of the old, and having freed them from the shackles of feudalism and imperialism. The old China was remarkably devoid of trees.

The large, modern Min Zu hotel, several storeys high, is on the Chang An Jie, the Street of Eternal Peace, which has been driven right through the middle of Peking from east to west, is over 40 metres wide, and 48 kilometres long, and passes right through the Tian An Men square or Gate of Heavenly Peace, the heart of modern China. One of the first things to catch the eye on entering the hotel is a large panel of neon lights proclaiming that "China has friends all over the world."

Mr. Wang and I both checked in, and I noticed that we were next door to each other. "Who is this man?" I wondered, imagining he might be the Chinese equivalent of a KGB man. He had a fair command of English, and when he bid me goodnight, said we would discuss tomorrow's programme in the morning. Did I want to eat in the foreign or Chinese restaurant? I said the foreign, to start with.

The bedroom was light and airy, looked out over the Chang An Jie, had its own bathroom, and was provided with the usual refreshments common to all hotels, and put out at all meetings or conferences—a small tin of tea, some cigarettes and an enormous, beautifully decorated thermos of boiling water. Did the room have listening devices or was the telephone tapped? I needn't have bothered to think of these refinements. "Bugging" is an extremely sophisticated operation, and it was unlikely that the Chinese, with their present knowledge of technology, would trouble to install it in an hotel. Telephone books, of course, are not available to the public in communist countries, so I needn't have bothered on that score, unless someone chose to ring me. It took me some time to lock the door before turning in; if we turn the key clockwise in a right-hand lock, the Chinese turn it anti-clockwise to lock the door. In many ways they act differently from us, but they have given up the practice of opening a book at the back, and reading down, starting at the top of the right hand column.

At about six o'clock I dreamily woke to the sound of tooting motor horns, which is a feature of all Chinese cities, indeed of the country in general. A light toot indicates a bicycle too near the vehicle, or trespassing on the centre of the road, a long drawn out one a near miss. And yet, in spite of the dense traffic on the Chang An Jie, I never saw an accident on it. The traffic steadily builds up, and by 7.30 am, both sides of the great street are filled with what looks like a gently floating mass of humanity—China going to work on bicycles. Peking has a population of nearly eight million and is said to have over five million bicycles.

Down in the "foreign" dining room, big by any standards, there were small round tables at one end, and much larger rectangular ones at the other, these being for the tourist groups of the various nationalities, and marked with cards accordingly, France, Brazil and Greece, I think. Mr. Wang meanwhile was regaling himself in the Chinese dining room.

Young waitresses, all identically dressed in white blouses, rather ill-fitting blue trousers, and black slippers, with hair arranged in one or two plaits, glided noiselessly about, as I took my place at one of the smaller tables. The Chinese idea of a foreign breakfast is an egg dish of some kind, very hard toast, coffee or tea and a tiny portion of butter and jam. Wherever you go, the butter portion is always of the same size, and the jam (referred to by them as "jim") always of the same colour, texture and taste. Occasionally one or two small sweet cakes are provided.

After breakfast I met Mr. Wang in the foyer, and told him I would like to send off a few postcards before settling down to the serious business of the programme for the day. A postcard from Peking to relatives and friends is a must, and greatly appreciated, particularly at this time, when a visit to China was still something of a novelty. Stamping the postcards was an unexpected problem, as the Chinese do not seem to have mastered the art of applying adhesive to their stamps, a pot of glue being provided at the reception desk for use by visitors.

Most of the sights and attractions of Peking and the surrounding countryside were well known to me from one and a half years residence there from 1928 to 1930. As Mr Wang and I, however, sauntered down the great new Chang an Jie towards the Tian An Men, more and more changes became apparent. "The population of Peking has surely grown a lot since Liberation judging by the enormous crowds on the streets", I said. "Oh, yes" replied Mr. Wang "it has quadrupled since 1949, and is now about eight million, second only to Shanghai. In addition to being the capital, it has become an important industrial centre. All those blocks of flats you see in the distance are for industrial workers. There was a time when buildings were not allowed to exceed the height of those in the Imperial Palace, but this rule has long since been forgotten. It was this rule which gave Peking its flat, rather low profile."

One noticed particularly the extreme standardisation of clothing for both sexes, the men wearing Mao-type blue outfits and caps and the girls all wearing trousers, mostly blue in colour, with their hair done in plaits. One evening I saw a football match televised, the spectators, in the stands presenting a background of solid blue. Occasionally a soldier in his baggy green uniform with red star in the cap and red collar tabs, or a small party of colourfully dressed children from a kindergarten, would break the monotony. From time to time an old woman with bound feet would hobble along, a practice long since outlawed and one of which today's generation feels very ashamed. Where gay and colourful banners used to advertise the names of the shopkeepers

Bicycles, bicycles

and what they sold, there is now no indication of what a shop deals in, for they are all government owned, the wages of the shop assistants and the prices they can charge for goods equally the province of the Government. Only the bookshops seemed to be well stocked, tidy and well organised. Many of the food shops stay open all night.

Traffic on the Chang An Jie was light by Western standards with large numbers of bicycles, overfilled buses, a few private cars, push carts and an odd pedicab. Rickshaws have been banned entirely. No Chinese citizen is allowed to own a private car, which is the preserve of officials or authorised organisations. In spite of the milling crowds, the flotillas of bicycles and the constant horn tooting, I never saw a single accident during the whole of my stay in Peking. Woe betide the foreigner who becomes involved in an accident in which a Chinese is killed or injured; two foreigners, one an Australian and one an American, had been held back for months in this connection.

Transport facilities have not kept up with the enormous increase in population, the two-coach single decker buses being crowded to the roof at most times of day. Police only operate at important road intersections and it is surprising to find so little traffic control in a country so highly organised in other respects. For most men and women going to work the bicycle is the best means of transport; it may cost the equivalent of five or six weeks wages, but this is less than the car equivalent in the West.

It took about half an hour to reach the Tian An Men square, the heart of the People's Republic, where in earlier days millions gathered to be addressed by Chairman Mao; during the Cultural Revolution there were no less than eight parades of Red Guards, each of more than a million. The square is vast and dominated by the Gate of Heavenly Peace, from where the leaders review parades from a rostrum rather reminiscent of that above the Chinese Wall on the Red Square in Moscow. There is a song in praise of the square and gate called "I love the Tian An Men" which is frequently sung by children in schools and kinder-gartens. When foreign dignitaries come to visit the Chinese leaders, the square and its approaches along the Chang An Jie are festooned with flags and bunting, a welcoming crowd being turned out to line both sides of the street, its number varying according to the importance of the visitor. The Chinese are past masters at handling large crowds of human beings, the task being simplified by the existence of street and neighbourhood com-mittees all over the city.

"Tell me about all these new buildings surrounding the square" I said to Mr. Wang "as they are all new since I was last here." "Those two long, low buildings facing you are the Hall

An acrobatic show

of Chinese History and the Hall of the Chinese Revolution; the tall plinth beside them is the Memorial to the Heroes of the Revolution with a message on the front of it in Chairman Mao's handwriting worded 'The People's Heroes are Immortal' and a message on the back of it in Zhou En Lai's handwriting worded 'The People's Heroes who laid down their lives in the War of Liberation and the People's Revolution in the past three years are immortal': round the base of the plinth there are eight carved plaques, each illustrating events in China's recent history which have led up to final Liberation in 1949. The first depicts a chest of opium being taken off to be burnt in 1840 when your countrymen were pouring the drug into our country to the detriment of our peoples health. Behind you is the Great Hall of the People built inside ten months in 1958, in which every province has its own reception room furnished with its own products; the theatre, which is used for meetings of the National Peoples Congress and other important bodies, can seat 5,000 people, a feature of it being a giant cluster of lights over the auditorium which portray a beautiful sunflower when illuminated. The banqueting hall can seat 5,000 or provide a buffet supper for 10,000." We went into the building and visited the reception rooms of Hunan, Sichuan, Liaoning and Guangdong provinces, all exquisitely and beautifully furnished. Facing the Tian An Men on the opposite side of the square I recognised the Qian Men, one of the gates in the old city wall, part of which has been left standing on each side of it, the main city wall having been demolished to improve the flow of traffic.

Foreign visitors are regaled with evening performances of Peking opera, ballet, concerts, films and acrobatics and I was certainly no exception. "We are going to see a performance of a Peking opera this evening", said Mr. Wang. "The White Haired Girl" the name given to the opera, had been a domestic servant in the house of a landlord in Sichuan province in southwest China, where she was so badly treated that she one day disappeared, to be discovered years later living wild in the mountains by a roving band of revolutionary guerrillas; in spite of her youth her hair had gone grey from privation and exposure to the elements. She joined the guerrilla band and guided them to the house of the landlord who had maltreated her; a battle ensued between the Kuomintang (Chiang Kai-shek's men) and the guerrillas in which the former were defeated and the landlord captured. He dived on to the stage in a splendid display of acrobatic skill and somersaulting, to be despatched there and then by a burst from a tommy gun. This was the forerunner of many other performances with a similar revolutionary theme. Peking opera might be described as a cross between theatre and opera in the Western sense, with a good deal of dancing and acrobatics thrown in. Jiang Qing, wife of Chairman Mao, was at this time at the height of her power as the custodian of his revolutionary outlook in the field of art and literature; artists had to work within very narrow limits and at all times stress the revolutionary message, which resulted in the constant repetition of the same theme.

During the honeymoon period between Russia and China from 1950 to 1960 a good many theatres of standard design were constructed in the main cities. They take audiences of up to 3,000, the seats all being at one low standard price. On each side of the stage there are narrow vertical lighted boards, which during the singing items show illuminated Chinese characters to enable the patrons to follow the wording of the songs. Each theatre has a sitting-out room for VIPs where tea and cigarettes can be served to members of the audience during the intervals. If the accommodation provided for the audience is somewhat austere, this is more than balanced by the backdrops on the stage, which are full of colour and beautifully designed. Acting is no longer a monopoly of men as it used to be in old China, when all the female parts were played by them.

A party of foreigners was present at the performance, suitably shepherded by two officials of the China International Travel Service who sat at each end of their row as if to segregate them as far as possible from the locals. At the end the foreigners filed out in a body; none of the Chinese in the theatre moved until the foreigners had left. The opera had started at 7.30 pm. and finished well before 10 pm., when everything closes down. The Chinese are early bed-goers and equally early risers.

At another time we went to a ballet performance, the first part of which depicted life in a village before the revolution, with landlords and gentry managing its affairs. After the revolution the village became part of a commune, which was unsuccessfully attacked by the previous landlord; he was captured and immediately despatched in the usual manner. The *Yellow River Concerto* which we went to on another occasion was played partly by Western and partly by Chinese instruments with a not displeasing result, except that the drums and clashing cymbals sometimes completely drowned the harmonies.

I noticed in the theatres that men seemed to predominate in the audiences, which prompted me to ask Mr. Wang whether young couples and husbands and wives often went to shows together. He said that this was difficult—in his own case for instance his wife worked in a chemical factory and their young daughter aged five was in a boarding kindergarten, so that they only came together on a Sunday, if they were both free from

Children in a kindergarten

work. It was interesting that he mentioned Sunday, which officially equates as a working day no different to the other six. Family life has come under great strain, not only because of the Government's directive that loyalty to family is secondary to loyalty to the state, but because of long separations of husbands and wives due to conscription, transfer to other jobs and other factors; a married woman wears no wedding ring and keeps her maiden name after marriage, which is confusing to Westerners.

Our first visit to a boarding kindergarten was an enlightening and enjoyable experience. The woman in charge was aged 34 (most people in responsible jobs seemed to be in the 30 to 40 age group) and she had rehearsed two small groups to put on shows for our benefit. The first comprised a small party of girls beautifully attired in colourful Mongolian costumes who danced to music under the supervision, as it were, of a young boy dressed as a soldier with a wooden rifle, who constantly kept wagging his forefinger at them as they danced round him in a circle. It transpired that they were supposed to be guarding a sheep commune in Inner Mongolia and that the soldier was warning them to look out for landlords who might steal the sheep, or capitalists/imperialists who might attack the commune. Another little party of younger children sang the praises of the communes.

The schooling of young children from the age of two or three is highly developed and universal; the age question is complicated by the fact that Chinese babies are rated as being one year old at birth. A child born to a factory worker will probably first be looked after in a creche there; if the factory is large, it may also run a kindergarten as well. Some of the boarding kindergartens charge a small fee, but this is not general. Street committees also run kindergartens—it all depends on the location of large numbers of small children. One thing common to them all is the indoctrination into the Communist way of life. Reading, story telling, playlets or acting have a high political content.

With mothers working and parents frequently separated for long periods, children don't see much of their mothers in the early stages of their lives. Lucky indeed are those families which can count on the help of a granny; she is a very important pillar of society. The end product of the kindergartens is highly disciplined, well behaved and not given to vandalism, quite apart from being loyal to the institutions of the State.

"Where do the foreign diplomats live?" I asked Mr. Wang. When I lived in Peking before, they used to have embassies in what was called the Legation Quarter, which was the scene of much fighting at the time of what we called the Boxer Rising in 1900, when peasants calling themselves the "Society of Harmonious Firsts" fought against the foreigners and reckoned they were impervious to the bullets fired by foreign rifles. I'm rather surprised there isn't a plaque dedicated to the Boxers on the Memorial to the Heroes of the Revolution."

"Oh yes, I know all about that", Mr. Wang said. "All the old embassies have been taken over by the Government for administrative purposes and what you knew as the Peking Club is now used for putting up students from Third World countries. The foreign embassies are now all in new buildings in an area facing the Chang An Jie not far beyond the Tian An Men. Some of the foreign journalists live there too and quite close by is a large three storied Friendship Shop exclusively for the use of the foreign community. We've always had to keep a close eye on foreigners, you know."

The China International Travel Service (or CITS) had very kindly given me the use of a car and chauffeur for the duration of my stay in Peking; it was a "Shanghai" saloon, a little out of date and not very fast, but entirely reliable, and made in the city of its name. We, (that is Mrs. Li, Mr. Wang and I) decided to take a trip out to the Shih San Ling, the Thirteen Tombs of the Ming dynasty emperors (1368–1644), situated about 40 kilometers north of Peking. The immediate approach to the tombs is along an avenue of stone animals, some true to life and some mythical, 24 in all, ending with 12 mandarins in stone, six on each side of the avenue. Facing the visitor on arrival is the

Hall of Eminent Favours, with its yellow glazed tile roof supported by 32 colossal wooden pillars, sited in front of the Chang Ling, the tomb of the first Ming emperor to be buried here inside a huge round tumulus; in front of the tomb are sited a stele or upright pillar and an altar, at which later emperors prayed for their ancestor.

One of the tombs, the Ding Ling, has been opened up in recent years. You walk down a short road, walled on both sides and enter the many chambered burial hall, filled with all the objects and treasures thought likely to be of use to the deceased in his after life. The emperor Wan Li and two of his wives were buried in this chamber, many of the dresses, garments, jewels and personal possessions of the latter having survived the test of time. While I was looking at some of the gold and silver plate, my eye suddenly caught sight of a large rectangular placard hanging from the roof of the chamber, which stated in bold English lettering that "The labour used in building this tomb would have kept one million people alive for six years." Having digested this information which I must say brought me sharply back to the present, whether I liked it or not, I continued admiring the host of other treasures until suddenly faced with another reminder of the infiltration of propaganda into this beautiful setting. On top of a chest were two plates, one quite small, of earthenware with no design and on it a small pile of rough gruel, the other of china with a beautiful design of birds, and much larger than the small one, and on it replicas of exotic fruit and fish. Between the two plates lay a card drawing attention to the starvation diet of the poor and the extreme luxury of the rich, and by implication the utterly feudal nature of China's past.

When we had left the tomb, I asked Mr. Wang why the Government thought it worth while perpetuating the memories of past Emperors. "I would have thought you would have wanted to forget them" I said. "Not at all—you've got it all wrong" he replied. "Those tombs are a memorial to the workers who built them by the sweat of their brows." It is not easy to better a dedicated communist in argument or debate. One would probably get the same answer if visiting the Tsarskoe Selo outside Leningrad.

We took a walk round the Forbidden City, now renamed the Imperial Palace, and found few changes since the days before the Liberation, except that the crowds were greater and the buildings better cared for. It was refreshing to see so many priceless treasures completely unguarded after the constant rattling of keys in public establishments in the West. I noticed one stall selling bottles of pop which was drunk on the spot, the empty bottles being returned for cash. Anything remotely resembling a luxury such as cigarettes or lemonade is heavily taxed.

The first industrial establishment we visited was a printing works employing 3,500 people and producing magazines, books and postcards. Here one saw at first hand the tremendous handicaps imposed by the nature of the language. Over 200 girls were laboriously setting type by hand, drawn from great banks of metal characters. The composing room takes up a great deal of space and any expansion of production involves adding additional banks of characters; it is difficult to visualise a linotype machine being used for a pictographic language like Chinese, but I was assured that experiments were being made with that in mind.

In one department I saw some quite young children working at a bench and being taught a production process in accordance with Mao's dictum that all young people must learn the meaning of manual work from a very early age. Some of the departments were festooned with "Da Zi Bao" or "Big Character Posters" hanging from the roof or fixed to the walls; any employee can write out and display one of these on any subject he or she likes, provided it is signed by the author. Where criticism of managers is concerned, I understand it is aired at open meetings.

Hours of work were 7.30 to 11.30 am. and 12.30 to 4.30 pm., a six-day, 48 hour working week. Every factory has a trade union which is an organ of government with the duties of improving production and production processes, of encouraging inventiveness and of ensuring that workers are loyal to the Communist Party, decisions about hours of work and rates of pay not being within its competence. The 48 hour week seemed to be universal, wage rates being controlled by the central government on the basis of eight degrees rising from about 30 yuan (or about £9) per month to a maximum of 120 yuan (or about £36 per month) with a very small number of specialists earning above that figure.

As I got to know Mr. Wang better we touched on more and more subjects, both economic and political. He simply could not understand the frequent changes of leadership in the democratic countries and firmly believed that all the politicians in the West were dishonest and corrupt. He seemed to think that constant changes of leadership were a sign of decay in our society. I told him I thought it strange that his Government had sent an official invitation to ex-President Nixon who had been removed from office for the very faults he had mentioned. "We like Nixon" he replied "and we don't believe he is any more corrupt than any of the other Western politicians. We like your people but heartily dislike your rulers." He was 38 years old and had of course only known a Communist regime and its picture of the outside world.

The tentacles of the Communist Party reach down to the very roots of society in both town and country. The neighbourhood committee in the larger town corresponds with the commune in the country, both being the lowest organisations directly responsible to the Government. Every street has its street committee responsible to the neighbourhood committee and it looks after the welfare and loyalty to party of every citizen in that street. Care of the old and young is its responsibility; it may run a kindergarten or small workshop for the use of the older citizens and housewives. I saw one party of pensioners doing flower paintings and decorating eggs for export. There will be a first aid clinic in the street, possibly a shop and even a restaurant. The committee I visited staged a kindergarten playlet, in which a bevy of young girls sang while they filled their baskets with gleanings from the fields after harvesting. This is normal practice in China where nothing goes to waste. Every scrap of animal dung is collected for manure and teams are appointed to collect the dung on roads used by horses, donkeys and mules.

Shops were very crowded; many of the food shops stay open all night. The unit of purchase is very small and housewives like to see their purchases weighed out. Comparatively few foodstuffs are in tins or packets. Why pay extra for fancy wrappings? Much of the shopping is done in the open markets selling vegetables, eggs, fish and poultry, which start business at about 6 am and are always thronged with buyers. Live ducks, geese and fowls have their necks wrung on the spot after purchase and are often plucked in an incredibly short time after immersion in boiling water. Prices, for vegetables particularly, are very low—cabbage at 2 pence per kilo, salt 2½ pence, flour 3 pence, meat 17 pence, eggs, 18 pence per dozen, two boxes of matches for 1 pence. Customers are honest to a degree, which made one Western entrepreneur think that supermarkets would do well. He might have saved the cost of pilferage, but he hadn't reckoned on the weighing out requirement, the cost of which would have more than counterbalanced any savings due to the absence of pilferage. The Chinese are great readers and the bookshops seemed better appointed than most. Everything is of course at fixed prices, even the curios and handicraft articles in the Liu Li Chang, the small street containing most of the art shops. Anything over a hundred years old carries a red seal and every item is marked with a price.

On another occasion we went out to visit a commune just outside Peking. This and other visits to organisations followed a strictly standardised pattern. The car drew up at the head office of the organisation; Mr. Wang and I got out and a gentleman stepped forward from a waiting group, who would be introduced as, say, "Mr. Li, Vice-Chairman of the Revolutionary Committee" no indication being given of the nature of his function within the organisation. It had been decided during the Cultural Revolution that all organisations should be run by revolutionary committees, each of which should contain a representative of the Communist party, of the workers and of the technicians; every organisation seemed to have a number of vice-chairmen.

We sat down in a committee room where tea and cigarettes were provided and, after some words of welcome, one member of the committee would give details of the number employed, the work done, the output and so forth. In a great number of cases production figures dating back to a period just prior to Liberation would be given to demonstrate the enormous increase in output, the base figure relating to a period of civil war and chaos in the country and as such being unreliable. Invariably what I would call the national "Topic of the Day" would be introduced, which at this time was the "Lin Biao—Confucius" theme (Lin Biao, designated as successor to Mao Ze Dong, was killed in an aeroplane crash in mysterious circumstances supposedly on his way to Russia. Confucius is regarded by the Communists as a conservative and one who favoured the establishment in his time. The implication was that Lin Biao was not a true revolutionary in the Mao tradition and had probably been plotting to kill him).

The commune, which I had always visualised as a purely agricultural productive enterprise, is in fact almost a small state within the state, carrying out the functions of a local authority in the West, as well as being an agricultural concern. The governing body is the commune committee headed by an elected chairman, while the productive units are the brigades and production teams of up to 20 who are paid by "work points". The head of the brigade is the brigadier, whose province probably covers a whole village, who is responsible for allocating tasks to the leaders of the production teams and whose job it is to ensure that the production targets laid down by the commune are met. Apart from the agricultural production, the commune is also responsible for any schools or hospitals within its area.

At our meeting we were given the following details of the commune we visited. Area—6,000 hectares, number of households—11,000, number of inhabitants—47,000, number of brigades—21, number of production teams—152, number of shops—56. There was also a small foundry, a brick kiln, hospital and several primary schools. The commune grew a hundred

Ducks on a Peking commune

different varieties of vegetable for the Peking market, this being
its main task; it produced additionally 20,000 pigs and 180,000
ducks per year.

The commune is a tidy organisation, increasingly devoting its
activities to forms of production other than agriculture. In old
China each village was virtually a law unto itself; during the
slack winter months its inhabitants may have gone in for handicrafts but were mostly without much work. The new organisation
makes it possible for major projects of road making and irrigation
to be carried out by pooling the labour resources of several
communes.

We visited the commune hospital, where both Chinese and
Western medicines were dispensed, and one of the duck farms
where the birds are forcibly fed and are ready for killing in the
incredibly short time of 60 days. A young boy was employed at
this farm whose sole duty it was to ram a pellet down the throat of
each duck as it waddled past in a procession, a very monotonous
job. I asked the man in charge whether the boy had volunteered
for the job or been directed to it. "Young Li is there to feed the
ducks" was the reply I got. It reminded me of a party of Chinese
musicians who played at the Edinburgh Festival and were
subsequently taken on a bus trip through the Highlands of
Scotland; as we travelled south amidst the magnificent scenery

of the Cairngorm mountains I turned to the man sitting opposite me and said, "What do you think of our countryside, Mr. Wu, compared to yours round Peking?" "It's different" came the answer and that was that.

When I got back to the commune, I asked to see the private plot of one of the workers, which turned out to be one of 96 square metres, on the basis of 48 square metres for each member of a family. The size, indeed the very existence of private plots, is a hotly contested subject between Left and Right, the former advocating either the complete abolition of the plots, or at least the merging of them into communal plots for several families, the latter advocating more land for private cultivation and the extension of markets for privately grown produce. Statistics· indicate that there has been a larger increase in the production of items associated with private plots, such as fowls, eggs, pigs, vegetables and fruit, than of staple crops such as wheat, maize, rice, millet and sorghum.

While I was out for most of the day, I usually had breakfast and dinner in the hotel and found myself on one occasion sitting next to a Swiss subject, who proved to be the representative of the entire Swiss watch industry. He had been making annual visits for the past twenty years, knew intimately the members of the trading corporation with which he had to deal and believed he would get his usual order to the value of one million Swiss francs per month, though things were getting more difficult, as the Chinese improved the quality of their own product. He stressed the importance of personal relations with the members of the trading corporation with which he was dealing; mutual understanding and good faith were vital in dealing with the Chinese.

Expenditure of foreign currency is strictly controlled and restricted to what the Chinese believe to be essential to the modernisation of their country; foreign food, wines and spirits do not come within that category, and visitors in the know usually bring with them items such as whisky or gin, bottles of which can be seen on the tables, labelled with the names of the owners. You sit at Table A one evening, leave your bottle of whisky on the table when you have finished dinner, return the next evening and find the table occupied by someone else with your bottle still on it. I had this experience with two Frenchmen, who willingly handed over my bottle of whisky, a tot of which I gave to each of them as a reward for looking after the bottle. Incidentally the Chinese produce something in a bottle which they describe as whisky; I bought a bottle of it to take home. Analysis proclaimed it to be peach brandy!

In spite of English being the chosen language in nearly all

the schools, very few English books are imported. I asked Mr. Wang what he would like me to send him when I got home and he immediately replied, "Oh please send me some books in English—we have practically none at the headquarters of the CITS."

On the top floor of the hotel there was a hairdresser. He had just started cutting mine, when a woman came in and occupied the seat next to me. "Hair dos" and "Hairdressing appointments" did not figure at all in a woman's life at this period of extreme puritanism. Plaits or at most a bobbed head were universal.

Much of the restaurant was occupied by Frenchmen who were staging an industrial exhibition in the city. Rumour had it that the exhibition was inside a large plastic dome, that no provision had been made for air conditioning and that the heat inside it was unbearable. Each of the major industrial nations is given in turn the opportunity of staging its own exhibit, to which much prestige is attached.

Having spent a night on the Great Wall many years previously I had become rather blasé about it, although its sheer size and length never fails to astonish me. Whereas in the old days it was visited by small groups of foreigners, it has now become a major attraction for thousands. Mao was still advocating the "export" of Chinese style revolution, and wooing Third World countries, particularly in Africa, where the Tanzam railway had been built in Tanzania, largely by Chinese labour, and in the Sudan where a hospital complex had been constructed. It was not surprising therefore to see a football team from Uganda and a basketball team from Nigeria walking up along the Wall. Since then the picture has changed dramatically, as the emphasis is on tourists from Western countries as a means of accumulating foreign currency in aid of the "Four Modernisations" programme; a special luxury train makes the daily trip to and from Peking carrying a thousand tourists. Pragmatism has taken the place of idealism; the Right has overcome the Left for the time being.

Always be prepared for the unexpected in China. One day Mr. Wang said to me, "I want you to come and visit one or two shops with me". We walked into the first one which was selling cloth and as we were standing at the counter, to my amazement the floor behind it started sliding away into the wall behind it, to disclose a flight of stone steps leading down to what I assumed to be a basement. "Come on down" he said "We are going to investigate". We found ourselves in a narrow, well-lit underground passage, along which we proceeded for two or three minutes, until we reached a spacious, well-appointed room with tables and chairs, in which there were two men and a girl of some 20 years of age. After the usual welcome and provision of tea and cigarettes, the young woman was asked to explain where we were. She said that we were in part of the air raid shelter system which embraced the whole of the centre of the city, had been built at nights, largely by volunteers, when there had been a threat of war with Russia in 1969, and was calculated to protect the citizens from nuclear bomb blast and fall-out. I said that in Great Britain we had had much experience of air raid ahelters in the war against German fascism and that in London the underground railway tunnels had provided shelter for thousands of people who spent whole nights sleeping on the platforms of the stations; these tunnels were a good deal deeper below ground than the ones we were in. Much was being said at that time about a new underground in Peking, but there has been nothing to indicate its completion—perhaps it is to form part of the city's defences. The object of the exercise was undoubtedly to convince the foreign visitor that they were well aware of the dangers of war and were doing their best to anticipate it.

The handicrafts industry is a considerable earner of foreign currency. In old China this was largely a cottage industry, in which individuals used their special talents. Shortly after Liberation steps were taken to draft individual craftsmen into small factories, which enabled their experience to be pooled and more attention to be paid to research and design on a bigger scale. In old China the individual craftsman had a precarious livelihood and the new arrangements have ensured a steady wage and employment for him or her. In many fields mechanical aids have been introduced and in one craft shop what looked like dentist's drills were being used in the production of carved ivory pieces, jade and amber. I don't think the results reached the standards of the old individual craftsmanship but they were none the less adequate in a world suffering in quality from mass production. We were shown one magnificent ivory piece which had taken ten people six months to complete.

Age old processes were not being neglected. One shop was using wooden printing blocks patiently carved by hand, a process handed down from the Tang dynasty (618–906). The prints taken from these blocks were exquisite and lacking in the hard outlines seen in prints mass produced from metal plates. Some quite young girls were employed on the carving process, which prompted me to ask once again whether they had volunteered for the work or been directed to it. "A bit of both" came the answer. "The girls come here from middle school with a recommendation from teachers as having a flair for the arts."

Retail shop in a commune

Apprenticeship is a long one, lasting several years.

In a previous chapter I wrote about the great tourist attractions such as the Imperial Palace, the Temple of Heaven, the Summer Palace, the Ming Tombs and the Great Wall and have mentioned them but little in this chapter, except in the case of the Ming Tombs where political capital has been made out of the opened tomb of Ding Ling. Generally speaking all these monuments to China's past have survived the years of chaos, Japanese invasion and civil war intact and have been well looked after by the Communist Government; much remains to be done; many of China's priceless treasures still remain under the ground, where new finds of historical and artistic interest are constantly being made.

VI
Shijiazhuang and
Tientsin, 1974

TRAIN journeys, anathema to travellers in the 1930s, are now a pleasure. The trains, if not very fast, run to time; the service is good, the compartments spotlessly clean and the food in the dining cars excellent. Every compartment has its damask curtains, tin of tea and thermos filled with boiling water, frequently refilled by the dining car attendants, usually quite young girls. Foreigners particularly are indulged by being given seats in the second class compartments, from which Chinese are for some reason frequently ejected; it is not clear whether this is due to difficulties of communication, simply to politeness, or to the risk of Chinese passengers being infected by foreign democratic ideas or what. For some reason there is an aversion to the citizens being exposed to contacts with foreigners.

In the early 1900s, when China was a happy hunting ground for foreign entrepreneurs, concessions for building railways were given to various foreign companies. There was no clear cut overall national plan for railway construction and before Liberation there were three entirely separate railway termini in Peking. Now there is one newly built and finely equipped terminus for all routes, to which we repaired for the journey to Shijiazhuang, distant some 250 kilometres. The new station is on two floors with a moving staircase connecting the marble ground floor with the one above it, both of them of course milling with enormous crowds. As a foreigner I was privileged to bypass all the queues and pass right along the platform to a second class coach just behind the engine, which was a coal burning steamer. It blew its whistle before starting and it was quite an experience to see and hear again the escape of hissing steam, the rattle of the coal being shovelled into the boiler by the stoker and the plumes of smoke passing by the window as we sped through the country side.

Mr. Wang had brought with him a chess set—quite a simple one made by the boys in a primary school—and he tried to teach me the game. Though the pieces have quite different names to ours (I remember one, being called a "pao", or "gun"), the moves are not dissimilar. As a pupil, however, I was a failure, as I couldn't understand the finer points of the game. The chess set was put away and we relapsed into silence.

After some time Mr. Wang suddenly leant across to me and said in a conspiratorial fashion, "Mr. Lo, I have a very difficult and confidential question I want to ask you. What is your income?" I had no idea why he wanted the information—presumably to reach some conclusions about the relative standards of living in China and the West. Whatever the reasons, I did my best to oblige him. "I worked for a large tobacco concern for over 30 years" I said, "and during every month of my long service with that company a small deduction from my salary was made towards my eventual pension, when I retired. The company made a matching contribution from its profits and these arrangements were made for everyone in the employment. As a result they now pay me an annual sum of over £4000 pounds until I die. In addition during the long period of my employment I was paying a small sum each month to the Government, which qualified me for a national pension, amounting to some £800 per annum. I have some additional income from dividends on capital paid from the profits made by companies in which I have shares, so you might say that my gross income amounts to about £6,000 per annum. I say gross, because this is what I receive before taxation which removes a considerable part of it."

As the tale of my income grew, I could see his eyes opening ever wider with astonishment. "You are extremely rich" he said at last, when I had finished.

I then tried to explain to him some of the intricacies of our taxation system. "In the first place" I said "my pensions are subject to income tax (there is no tax on earned incomes in China). I couldn't give you an exact figure of what the deduction for income tax might be—probably something like £800 or £900 per annum. Then there are innumerable other taxes; I have to pay for a licence for my car and T.V. If I want to shoot game I have to take out a licence—even the ownership of a dog attracts a small contribution. Wines, spirits and cigarettes are all heavily taxed, and then I have to pay rates, which are a form of local taxation on my house. Over and above all that I have by law to insure my car, the petrol for which is also heavily taxed. There are numerous other taxes which I won't go into now."

As the list lengthened he became more and more confused with the intricacies of my financial arrangements and finally burst out, "Your life in the West is far too complicated—I am very glad that I live in China, where life is simpler, money an irrelevance and citizens spend their time serving other people and the State". I discovered later that the combined income of him and his wife, who worked in a chemical works, was about 96 yuan or dollars per month, equivalent to about £28 pounds, which was spent roughly as follows. Food £12, fee for boarding out their five-year-old daughter at a kindergarten £5. Clothes £3, bus fares 70p, heat and light 50p, rent 40p, sundry £1.40, leaving unspent £5. All taxation is indirect and might be involved in clothing. Taxation on food is levied on the communes on the basis of the amount of food they sell to the state. Any savings can be banked, at a small rate of interest between one and two per cent according to the length of deposit, or could be saved up to buy a bicycle, watch, radio or sewing machine, these being the four most popular items in demand. Comparisons between the standard of living in China and the West are very difficult, partly because of the virtual absence hitherto of inflation in China, and partly because of the extreme cheapness of some of the basic foods.

The same countryside which I had passed through in the train in 1930 had not changed outwardly to any marked degree. Contrary to what was said in the Western press in 1958 when the communes were first formed, there has been no wholesale rehousing of the peasant population, which for the most part lives in the villages where it has alway lived. Trees line both sides of nearly all the roads, which have been considerably improved; not many tractors and lorries were to be seen on them, most of the traffic consisting of horse carts, push carts, a few wheelbarrows and bicycles. Production teams of up to twenty have taken the place of the odd individuals one used to see scattered about. Crops of wheat, maize, millet, sorghum and cotton are much what they used to be. Irrigation has obviously been increased and improved by the installation of electric pumps which is widespread; men working treadmills with their feet to keep the water moving along the trenches of the flat Hebei plain are no longer to be seen. Some of the newer houses were being built of kiln fired bricks and glass was beginning to replace rice paper on windows.

As we approached the outskirts of Shijiazhuang, I looked with astonishment at the factories and blocks of flats. A village of perhaps 10,000 souls and a small railway junction, when I had lived there, had grown into a large city with a population of 800,000 employed mainly in cotton spinning and the making, dyeing and finishing of cloth.

Three smartly turned out CITS men met us at the station, who took us to the modern hotel, where later a feast was staged in my honour. Details of the food have escaped me apart from the particularly delicious prawns. One of the CITS men spoke

Harvesting cotton near Shijiazhuang

no English and only knew Russian. He had been trained in that language during the 10-year friendship period, but now had no use for it, as there were no longer any customers. There must be many other interpreters who backed the wrong horse, as there were thousands of Sino-Soviet Friendship societies at that time. I have a little Russian myself and he was delighted to return to his own speciality for a short time.

Next morning we were off early by car to visit a small commune called Wa Feng Tai, about 90 kilometers distant. Tarmaced at first, the road got steadily worse as we progressed. Most of the traffic on it consisted of carts, some pulled by single horses or mules, others by every conceivable combination of draught animals, including in one case a combination of a donkey and a camel!

As we drew near to the headquarters of one of the brigades in the commune we saw in front of us a long white notice board, which must have measured at least 15 feet across by four feet in depth, carrying a message in large red Chinese characters which read, when translated, "Heartily welcome English friend". It was a touching welcome, which I thought must have come spontaneously from the people, as it had a very "home made" look about it. Standing beside the board were the chairman of the commune, the local brigadier and a girl of about 17 who proved to be a student sent down to the countryside to do her stint after leaving school. We went into the office for the usual refreshments and briefing and discovered that the brigade had on its own initiative built a completely new dam, to prevent flooding in winter and preserve water for irrigation in the summer, as well as breeding fish, a valuable source of protein for the commune. This part of China is very subject to extremes of flood and drought.

This was quite a small commune in the foothills of the mountains in Hebei province, the land being poor and unproductive except where terracing had been built on the hillsides to give a reasonably good depth of soil; the brigade we were visiting had only a hundred acres of arable land on which to grow grain crops; apples and nuts were grown on the hillsides. The dam had been built by some 160 men over a period of six successive winters without the help of any mechanical aids; it was about 20 metres high and 100 metres across. Quite close to it a production team was working, underplanting the growing wheat crop with maize, some of its members being quite young people doing their stint on the land after leaving middle school. On our way back to the headquarters we saw another tiny private plot growing vegetables. The brigadier said it had been laid down that no more than five per cent of the total arable land should be devoted to private plots.

We visited one house occupied by three brothers and their families, consisting of three wives and a total of seven children, four girls and three boys. They said they had suffered badly from the exploitation of landlords, and that at one time things had got so bad that they had had to sell a fourth brother to save them from starvation; then the Japanese had come to add to their difficulties. I asked one of the wives if she knew about birth control. She said she did and approved of it.

Before we left we were given an excellent lunch made up exclusively from their own produce and also a bag of nuts to take away with us.

Shijiazhuang and the surrounding area was the scene of much guerrilla fighting against the Japanese during the Second World War. The only pitched battle involving large numbers of troops on both sides was fought at Pingxinguan near a pass on the way to Taiyuan, the capital of the next door province of Shanxi. It is fitting therefore that there should be a Memorial Park to honour the memory of the many guerrillas who lost their lives in the neighbourhood. Inside the Park is a statue of Dr. Norman Bethune, a Canadian Communist doctor, who was with the anti-Franco forces in the Spanish civil war and subsequently with Mao's guerrillas; he carried out thousands of operations in the field before he himself died of blood poisoning

Coat made of coir used by a soldier on the Long March

in 1939. Little known outside China, he is one of the leading folk heroes of the Communist Party. There are smaller memorials to two Indian Communist doctors who worked with him.

Inside the Park there is a building dedicated to Dr. Bethune and the ingenuity and inventiveness of the guerrillas he served. In the eyes of the Western allies during the Second World War Chiang K'ai Shek was the acknowledged ruler of China and all military and economic aid was directed to him; apart from what they were able to capture from the Japanese or Chiang's forces Mao's troops had no modern weapons. The building contains an astonishing collection of makeshift weapons such as rifles, pistols, grenades and land mines, some of them primitive in the extreme. The ashes of some of the heroes of the war are interred in the building, the urns being set into the walls and named on small plaques. Relics and photographs of the epic Long March in 1934/5 were also on show.

I looked for my old headquarters in vain—it had been bombed by the Japanese.

We visited quite a large factory for dyeing, printing and finishing cloth, built in 1958, and producing a good quality article, much of it in floral patterns and everything subjected to a rigid quality control. The walls on both sides of the entrance were a solid mass of Chinese characters, exhorting workers to do this and do that, to pay regard to the quality of their work and to be loyal to the Communist Party. A notice in large characters above the entrance proclaimed "Everyone must learn from Daqing" this being the country's largest oil field in North Manchuria which the Chinese have developed almost entirely themselves.

Like many of the larger factories this one had its own kindergarten for its employees children. It also provided housing for many of its employees in large blocks of flats, one of which we visited. The family consisted of father and mother, two sons (one of them married with two children) a daughter and the daughter in law—a total of eight; the unmarried son and daughter lived elsewhere, leaving the remaining six to share the two bedrooms. Young people who get married almost invariably live with one or other of the parents; it is almost unheard of for a young married couple to set up on their own. The growth of population is such that the pressure on housing gets worse, rather than better; lucky are those who work in a factory which provides them with housing. As it seemed likely that the kitchen was being shared by the mother and daughter-in-law, I asked the former whether this ever led to controversy; she entirely failed to understand the question until I told her that in Western countries young married couples usually set up on their own after marriage, and that when they had to live with their in laws, this frequently led to friction. Shared kitchens and living accommodation is normal practice for young marrieds in China.

To finish off this delightful visit we were entertained in the evening by a party of children from a primary school, helped by some older children from a middle school. The show was staged in the hotel's theatre; some Canadians were staying in the hotel and, when they and I appeared in the theatre, the assembled actors and performers let out a great cry of "Huan ying, huan ying" or "Welcome, welcome". They danced and acted small playlets, the dancing being accompanied by their own orchestra; each item was announced by a young girl from the stage who was without shyness of any kind, though she could not have been more than 12 years old.

The rail journey to Tientsin involves returning to Peking which is about 130 kilometres away. It lies near the sea, was once a treaty port and in bygone days the second most important trading city next to Shanghai. The countryside we passed through between Peking and Tientsin was very dry, with vehicles churning up great clouds of dust behind them—a bad augury for the harvest, which means so much. China is better placed than she was with reserves of grain and better communications to distribute it to needy areas, but she can ill afford to import grain from abroad costing precious foreign currency. Improved irrigation has also reduced the danger of drought, always a menace to crops in North China.

Driving away from the station in a taxi we narrowly missed running down a man in the street, which might have had serious and quite unpredictable repercussions, even though we were only passengers in the vehicle. Mercifully he escaped without a scratch and we went on our way to the Astor House hotel, which was of old the stopping place for the leading taipans and business people visiting the then treaty port. There it still was in all its Victorian glory, with dark mahogany walls, brass bedsteads, enormous cast iron baths with large brass taps and equally solid radiators; the decor can hardly have been touched since before the outbreak of the Second World War. Few Chinese residents were to be seen and apart from the party of Canadians from Ottawa the only other foreigners were two German ladies from the West German Embassy in Peking; staffs of the embassies apparently have a limited freedom to travel about, accompanied by men from the CITS.

In the evening we went off to a local group's Peking opera production of *Battles on the Plain*, a saga of the war against the Japanese, who were eventually defeated after being misled by a ruse. It was thoroughly in keeping with revolutionary requirements and only remarkable for the astonishing acrobatic feats performed in battles between the two sides. There is surely no other nation capable of matching the Chinese in the field of acrobatics—they are brilliant.

The next day we had two factory visits, the first to a carpet factory, a traditional industry in North China and in Tientsin in particular. The tufting is hand-done by young women sitting on rather uncomfortable benches facing the backing for the carpet; designs are often intricate with flower or bird patterns, interspersed with characters standing for good luck, prosperity, long life and other good omens; the pile is particularly close and thick. After tufting the carpets are washed and shaved by electrically operated scissors. As always the blending of colours is perfect; there was one tapestry depicting horses in Mongolia which had over three hundred different shades of wool— a masterpiece. Much of their production is exported to 40 different countries. The factory had 1,300 workers, most of them living in modern flats owned by the firm. Female employees retire at 50 and males at 60 and we were told that the firm paid their pensions calculated at 70 per cent of their wage on retirement.

The second visit was to the large Number One Machine Tool Factory, with 13 separate workshops and 4,500 employees, of whom a quarter were women. The high proportion of women employed in engineering works is general and is immediately apparent on the shop floor, where many of the lighter jobs are done by them as well as the manning of the overhead cranes. I recently attended a lecture by a young British woman who had just returned from a visit to China and who was complaining bitterly about the lack of opportunities for women in the engineering industry in Britain.

The top manager of this large enterprise was quite a young man named Mr. Tui, who came in on his bicycle at 7.30 a.m. with all the other workers and was indistinguishable from them. We were told that he had been elected by his fellow workers; how far this was strictly true and how far he was the nominee of the Communist Party is difficult to assess. In their eyes the overriding requirement is complete loyalty to the party— knowledge of the job and factory processes are secondary considerations. "Red before Expert" and "Put Politics in Command" have been oft repeated dicta of Mao Ze Dong. Things may well have changed in this respect with the push for the "Four Modernisations" of agriculture, science and technology, industry and the armed forces since Mao's death. With hours of work and rates of pay laid down by the central government, no reward for extra productivity, very restricted

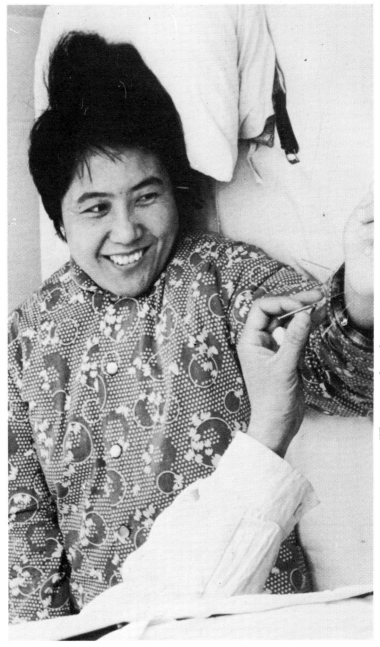

Woman undergoing acupuncture treatment

holidays and no pay for overtime, there seems little incentive to improve one's lot. All workers are there to "Serve the people".

Another feature of communist industry at plant level is the virtual absence of administrative offices, advertising, sales promoters, PROs and all those ancillary personnel additional to the production worker in the West. At this plant the ratio of staff and ancillary personnel to productive workers was one to 25. The bureaucracy is there of course in the shape of a large government staff far removed from the plant.

In every department you visited clapping immediately broke out and in some places I almost found myself clapping first, so infectious had it become. There was a large, plain, practical canteen serving cooked food and also providing facilities for workers cooking their own.

There was no end to the variety of the visits, the next one being to a 400-bed children's hospital, where a small boy was undergoing a stomach operation under acupuncture. There was a wire attached to each of his ears carrying a low voltage electric current; he uttered not a sound as the operation proceeded. Only his head was visible to me, so I could see no acupuncture needles.

A visit to a large middle school disclosed that fully 20 per cent of the pupils time was being spent on manual work—in this case they were making school desks. According to the headmaster of the school 47 per cent of Tientsin's population had been illiterate at the time of Liberation in 1949. In one of the schoolrooms there was an ancient and rather badly tuned piano, which I was invited to play. Thank goodness I had the "Moonlight Sonata" at my finger tips and was able to oblige.

Never a dull moment—in the evening yet another Peking opera. A woman has joined a detachment of Red soldiers. She knows the geography of a landlord's house and persuades the officer commanding the Red detachment to pose as a business man wanting to do business with the landlord. He duly calls and is admitted; meantime the woman, called Wang Jing Hua, steals in through the back door and shoots up the household. Fighting then breaks out with some Kuomintang troops who appear. After the battle is over Wang Jing Hua is reprimanded for being too precipitate in attacking the landlord's house.

Time was found to visit an art exhibition which was on three floors, divided between paintings and scrolls on the bottom floor, jade, coral, ivory, lacquer and other handicraft articles on the middle floor, earthenware and ceramics on the top floor. On most of the scrolls and paintings of post-Liberation origin politics have dictated the inclusion of tractors, power lines, railways and other modern subjects against the traditional backgrounds of mountains, lakes and other country scenes; the stark contrast between old and new is not a pleasing one. Jewellery and precious stones are less adaptable for political purposes, but again on the top floor there was a repetition of what we had seen in the opened Ding Ling tomb—a coarse earthenware plate exhibiting the starvation diet of the peasant set against a beautiful dish of choice fruit and sweetmeats as consumed by the rich. Art for politics sake has been taken to extremes.

In between times I had one or two verbal contests with Mr. Wang. "What is going on about inflation in your country?" he asked. "It seems to have got out of control and must be very hard on poorer people. Here we have not got such a thing; in fact the price of certain medicines was reduced only a few days ago".

"It is not such an embarrassment as you think," I replied. "By and large wages keep pace with inflation, in fact sometimes unfortunately exceed it. It is bad from a business point of view, as it tends to make the price of the goods we export uncompetitive in world markets".

"A thing I can't understand" I went on "is how you and the Soviet Union have fallen out, both nurtured on the wisdom of Lenin and Karl Marx, and believed at one time to be going to sweep the world together with your Communist principles. And here you are now at daggers drawn, even talking of war against each other. I simply don't understand it" After a short pause for reflection Mr. Wang drew himself up and said majestically "The Soviet Union has ceased observing the principles of communism as envisaged by Lenin and Karl Marx. It has become a Socialist/Imperialist power bent on world hegemony and is ruled by an elite which has lost all contact with the Soviet people".

There is no doubt about the hostility to Russia and the fear that they might be invaded. They regard the Russian soldiers as even more "li hai" or "savagely fierce" than the Germans were in the Second World War. If you raise the question of relations with the Soviet Union in the company of a gathering of Chinese, an awed hush seems to descend on the company and the subject is not pursued.

VII
Manchuria, 1974

TRAVELLING northwards in the train from Tientsin I was surprised to see quite a number of paddy fields, as one always associates rice cultivation with South China. In addition to the usual grain crops, apples and soya beans are grown. The train arrived at Shenyang, capital of Manchuria and previously known as Mukden, dead on time.

Shenyang is a well built modern city with a population of four million and a considerable stake in the engineering industry. Its development, and indeed the development of the whole of Manchuria, was carried out by the Japanese, who started investing in the country soon after their defeat of the Russians in the war of 1904–5; then in 1931 they occupied the country until 1945. For many years the Manchus resisted the immigration of Chinese from the mainland, which later became a flood owing to the disturbed conditions in China itself.

The modern hotel in the centre of the city faces on to the main square, which is dominated by an enormous statue of Chairman Mao surrounded by his revolutionary cohorts, the whole work being done in fibre glass (or "glass steel" as the Chinese call it). "Dong fang hong" or "The East is Red" is virtually the national anthem and we were not allowed to forget it, as there were two consecutive, very loud renderings of it on bells from a tower in the centre of the city at 6 a.m. A party of overseas Chinese was staying in the hotel; a Frenchman and I were the only foreigners. A small Friendship store was doing no business. A film *Azalea Mountain* following the usual revolutionary pattern was shown on one evening. It was all very quiet and dull; neither the Frenchman nor I had had any news of the outside world for at least 10 days.

First item on the programme was a visit to a 400-bed hospital with a staff of 1,300. Like some other large buildings it had been completed in 1958 the year of the "Great Leap Forward". A tooth was being extracted from an elderly male patient, pressure points being used during the operation, but no anaesthetics or acupuncture. In another section a girl, who had broken a leg in a bicycle accident, was lying on an operating table. There were a number of acupuncture needles in the leg to be reset, an operation carried out after the needles had been in position for about 40 minutes, after which the leg was bound up. Many patients treated by acupuncture are dealt with in the out-patients department and the Chinese claim that they have fewer patients using hospital beds than we do. The pharmacy carried a wide variety of Chinese medicines made up from roots, herbs, flowers and grasses, all labelled in Latin and Chinese.

Patients can opt to be treated by Chinese or foreign medicine. The course for doctors has been considerably shortened; an aspiring doctor, who may leave middle school at 16, will first go out to do his stint in a commune or factory for two or three years, and then go to university or a teaching hospital for another three. He learns far less theory than doctors in the West, which may be due to the urgent need to build up the medical services as quickly as possible.

A factory making "walking tractors", the workhorse of agriculture, had previously been making water taps. It had started making eight-horse-power machines in 1963 and was now making 12 horse-power ones. These all purpose tractors have a seat for the driver when pulling a trailer, handlebars for use when ploughing and a flywheel for driving stationary machines. They can also turn in a very small circle. Women accounted for a third of all the employees.

Just outside the city are the pretentious tombs of the first two Emperors of China's Qing or Manchu dynasty, who came from here; later Emperors were buried not far from Peking.

The CITS has an office in Shenyang and I saw there for the first time a young secretary typing on a Chinese type-writer; it is built on the same lines as a Western machine but instead of keys for each letter of the alphabet, numerals, punctuation marks, capital letters etc., there is a bed of over 3,000 characters facing the operator who has to work a claw-like device, which picks up the required character and applies it to the paper. One noticed from the ink marking on the characters in the bed that those most frequently used were in the middle. Each application to the paper of course represents the equivalent of a whole word; a qualified secretary should be able to type 40 characters or words per minute. I was told that the first typewriters were made by the Germans and Japanese, but that now they were being made by the Chinese themselves in Shanghai. It is quite a complex instrument and must demand a good deal more concentration than its English counterpart. The secretary was called Miss Liu; her parents lived 70 miles outside the city and she lived in a dormitory at the firm's office.

The boarding kindergarten we visited looked after 400 children aged three to six with a staff of fifty. They had a see-saw and laid on a tug of war for my benefit, neither of which I had previously seen in China. A highly disciplined body.

Fuxun with a population of 900,000 is within easy motoring distance of Shenyang and, as we motored through its suburbs, I caught a brief glimpse of some of the worst industrial housing I had ever seen in China, with shacklike buildings abutting on to unpaved streets covered in mud. Needless to say this did not form part of the scheduled visit which was to a home housing ninety old men averaging seventy five years of age, who for one reason or another had lost contact with their families or relations and were alone in the world. They came from different parts of China, slept three to a room on kangs, did a little gardening and weeding and played chess. They were about the only pensioners I saw anywhere who were not actively producing something; they were lucky to be there, as the home was out in the country, the food was good and the place well run. A small air raid shelter looked rather incongruous in such a peaceful setting.

Then a visit to a small factory making safety equipment for the mining industry—miners lamps, breathing apparatus, gas detectors and so forth. On one side of a room there was a comprehensive display of all their products, an open space being left in the middle of the display with two flaps which were dramatically opened when we reached it, to show an old fashioned piece of equipment said to have been left by the Russians as a prototype to be copied; in fact it was very out of date and its exhibition was intended to impress on us the untrustworthy nature of their former allies. They were very bitter about the way they had been left in the lurch by the sudden departure of the Russians in 1960.

The showpiece of Fuxun is the opencast coal and shale mine with a length of seven kilometres and a depth of some 240 metres, which has been operating since the early 1900s. The coal cut out at different depths from the walls of the mine is fed into trucks pulled by electric motors running on rails along the terraced sides of the mine, which produces three million tons of coal per annum, as well as shale for the production of oil. This information was given out at one of the usual introductory sessions, which was prolonged by the reading of pre-Liberation statistics, and the usual well-worn Lin Biao accusations. The Japanese had run the mine during their occupation of Manchuria and were accused of digging out all the best seams to the detriment of the workings in general. One man asked me if there was a right of search in our factories and I told him that in many factories there was such a right. He said that one of his friends had been caught stealing copper wire by the Japanese and had been given a prison sentence.

The Anshan Iron and Steel Co.

Next day we were off on our travels again by train to Anshan, an industrial city dominated by the huge Anshan Iron and Steel Company employing 150,000 workers in 67 different plants, of which we visited three, making seamless pipes, sheet steel and rails and girders. One had the impression that the number employed in all three plants was excessive, a factor common to all Chinese industry owing to the inexhaustible supply of labour. Chairman Mao had paid a visit to the firm some years previously and had given advice on the framing of the plant's constitution. The population of the city had grown from 200,000 to over a million since Liberation—in fact nearly every city we visited had populations above the million mark. Close by is an opencast iron mine run on similar principles to the coal mine at Fuxun with an iron ore crushing plant next to it. I had my first sight of a jeep made in Tientsin and named after it—quite a workmanlike, robust machine, in appearance not unlike its American counterpart.

I had an evening off and put down one or two notes about the sweeping changes brought about by the Communist regime. The emancipation of women and the requirement that they work has meant much more separation from their children, who in many cases spend the first five or six years of their lives in kindergartens and institutions rather than in the care of their mothers, unless there is a granny to look after them in their homes. This applies much more in the cities than in the countryside; city communications are poor and mothers often only see their children on their day off. In the eyes of the state loyalty to it and the communist party transcends all others considerations, a message firmly implanted in the minds of the children in their early formative years.

In a highly regimented society independence of thought or action is frowned on. "Serve the People" runs the writ and is the job of everyone. Aspirations to become airline pilots, cinema actors or any glamorous individual jobs are not encouraged; promotion at work involving an increase in salary is secondary to working for the good of the State. Wang frequently told me that "Money is an irrelevance in China" and that competitiveness and the urge to get to the top is a malaise in Western society, which is ruled by greed and acquisitiveness.

The longer one stayed in the country the more one became aware of the immense weight of propaganda and adulation surrounding the leadership, and Chairman Mao in particular. The dictates of the Communist Party are infallible; policies can change or be completely reversed overnight and the masses will follow them without a murmur. It is rare indeed, and probably dangerous, for an individual to express an opinion critical of the "official line."

Next morning off to the station to board a train for our last port of call at Dairen. Outside it a large party of children was drawn up and, as we drew nearer to them, the whole body suddenly started to clap—a sign of friendship for the foreigner. I was so taken aback that it took me a minute or two to return the greeting in similar fashion—one had come across this form of greeting by small numbers in factories, but never a mass display on this scale.

By this time I had two companions from the CITS, as Mr. Kao had joined us from their office in Shenyang. The number grew to three when we reached Dairen by the addition of Mr. Shao. The reasons for this were not clear to me, except that Dairen is a strategic place; perhaps they thought I should be particularly well watched.

Off we went to a beautifully situated modern hotel outside the city and close to the sea in a rather broken down old Russian built "Zim" car. There was a tunnel in a hillside on the way out and I was particularly asked to note that it was an air raid shelter. The hotel was practically devoid of visitors; I remember a most beautifully worked peony on the eiderdown on my bed and a very ancient wireless in a mahogany case, plus of course a splendid decorated thermos jug and a tin of tea. Still eating foreign food I had dinner alone in a small room.

Dairen, yet another city of over a million inhabitants, has a very modern appearance and has had a chequered history. Taken by the Japanese from China in 1894, when it was still quite a small town, it was handed over to the Russians in 1896 under protest, and as a result of pressure by the European nations, only to be taken back by the Japanese after their defeat of the Russians in the Russo-Japanese war in 1905. It remained in Japanese hands from then until their defeat in the Second World War, when the Russians again took it over, until it was handed back to China in 1952. It is not surprising therefore that the city has a distinctly Western appearance.

On the first evening we went to a theatre to see a second performance of the *White Haired Girl*, by which time I was getting tired of the Japanese/Capitalist/Landlord themes and asked to be excused in future from attending further performances of this kind; I had already seen seven.

On a visit to a school for deaf and dumb children it was a surprise to be greeted by a Vice-Chairman of the Revolutionary Committee in army uniform. The school had been started in 1950 by soldiers of the Peoples Liberation Army with seven or eight pupils and now had 400 and a staff of 50. There was a deafening noise in the classrooms as the children tried to follow

The Dairen Diesel Locomotive Works

their teachers in articulating words. Some of them were even trying to sing "Dong fang hong". After a round of the classrooms we were taken down to see a stage show by the children, in which songs entitled "I love the Tian An Men" and "Down with the Imperialists" figured prominently. The children were gaily dressed and acted well. Then on leaving the building the entire school turned out in their bright red tunics to bid us farewell, to the accompaniment of drums and clashing cymbals; it was a most rewarding and uplifting visit.

The Dairen Locomotive Works employed 8,000 people, of whom over 1,500 were women. Founded by the Russians in 1901 it changed hands twice before finally coming into Chinese ownership in 1952, when the outgoing Russians prophesied that the whole place would be overgrown in a few years time, and that the Chinese would be quite incapable of running it. In fact they have been remarkably successful in building a series of 2000-horse-power diesel locomotives for the state railways and had just started the production of a 4000-hp machine. Their locos had been running on the Mongolian section of the Trans Siberian Railway since 1964. It struck me as a well-organised concern producing excellent machines, in one of which I had a short ride.

I asked about the composition of the labour force and was told that 60 per cent of the employees were directed there by the central government on completion of their stint in field or factory, the remaining 40 per cent being trained in their own workshops. There was obviously a local tie-up with the Dairen University, which enabled them to recruit graduates from there direct. There must be local arrangements of this kind for many factories requiring skilled personnel. There are seven administrative regions in the country, but even at that level full direction of labour would be impossible.

Then came a nice surprise, for we were taken out for a sea trip by the harbour master in a fast tug. The harbour is a busy one, with a good many ships from Third World countries in the docks. In spite of what I was told about the extensive developments which had taken place, there were at least 15 ships lying off waiting to be unloaded. A good deal of oil is exported to Japan from here, most of it from the newly developed Daqing oilfield in Manchuria; a small tanker built in Dairen was pointed out to us. Outside the docks there was a club for foreign seamen which had its own Friendship Store.

The next day we had another short sea trip, this time on a small fishing vessel belonging to the Lu Da Fishing Co., situated some 30 kilometres from Dairen. It employed 5,800 people, some 3,000 of whom were seagoing fishermen, the remainder working on shore at ship repairing, landing and cleaning fish and operating a refrigerator plant. They worked an eight-hour day, except the women in the refrigerator plant who worked for only six hours. The company had a good export trade in herring roes and prawns, their vessels operating up to 500 miles away from base. They said that no fish were living within 30 miles of the Japanese coast owing to industrial pollution. A busy well managed place, with two quite young men in charge of it. Before we left we were given a gargantuan meal consisting entirely of fish caught by themselves, washed down with draughts of a powerful, locally distilled spirit.

That evening after dinner we had a good discussion about various topics of the day; Mr. Shao, our latest acquisition, unfortunately spoke no English, which slowed down the proceedings. I said that politics ought to be kept out of the lives of young children and that artists should be allowed freedom of expression, and not be bound by rules and regulations concerning the revolutionary content of their work. "Oh no" they said "Politics must be involved in every aspect of life; the rising generation must be made aware of the evils of the old society and not be given freedom to pursue their own ends, which results in selfishness and acquisitiveness, twin evils of capitalist

Grinding corn in a commune

society. All Chinese must learn to serve the people and the objectives of the Communist Party."

The conversation turned to foreign languages and I asked Wang if he had ever read any Shakespeare. "Oh yes" he replied "I was reading *Twelfth Night* only a few days ago."

"And what did you make of that" I asked.

"Far too many princes, dukes and duchesses, and not a word about the workers" he replied. The fact that it was descriptive of life in the 17th century and that the English was superbly written played no part in his judgement. Life for him and his contemporaries started in 1949. Poor Andrew Aguecheek and Toby Belch.

We went to yet another commune, or rather a brigade within a commune, with 1,100 households and a commune population of 37,000. The brigadier in charge was only 34 and was responsible for 16 production teams. It was a hilly area in a district subject to drought and a hillside had been laboriously terraced for planting apple trees. Water was pumped up electrically from ground level in two stages, with storage tanks at each level feeding irrigation channels. The main crops were wheat, maize and sorghum. There were 11 primary and three middle schools in the commune, and in the brigade we visited a speciality was the growing of tomatoes, lettuce, melons and vegetables out of season under polythene, which is increasingly being used in North China. These special crops were grown for sale in Dairen. The brigade had a well equipped workshop, with oxy-acetylene welding plant and a blacksmiths shop, and there was communication with every house in the village from the brigade's headquarters.

A most interesting place we visited in Dairen was a primary school with 3,000 pupils, divided between five primary and two middle school classes in the age groups from five to 13, with a staff of a hundred and up to 50 in each class. A quarter of classroom time was spent on the Chinese language with a requirement of 3,000 characters by age 13. Having been given all these particulars, with the usual addition of the Lin Biao-Confucius affair, a young girl of 12 got up behind a podium, and next to a chart of the city, and proceeded to describe in great detail the entire underground air raid shelter system, not only of the school, but of the whole city. It was an exercise similar to the one we had experienced in Peking but carried out by a much younger girl. In the case of the school she described the very primitive implements they used in the early stages of the exercise.

After this we walked over to a small hillside, in the side of which an entrance door led into the underground school, complete in every respect with desks, electric light, water and all services laid on in case of war. Next to the underground school there was a flat playground where a party of 25 pupils, girls and boys, were drawn up on parade carrying rifles with fixed bayonets. At a word of command they moved forward in single file to a row of firing points facing a row of metal plates set upright in the ground at a distance of 80 metres, and above them on a bank a row of balloons. The team lay down and firing started at the plates which were soon all knocked down, the finale being a concentration of fire on the balloons which all burst in a cloud of dust. One or two of the girls cannot have been more than 10 years old and had flowers in their hair; they were using service rifles, the bayonets of which protruded well above their heads when they stood to attention. I asked if there were any other military skills in the school and was told they had a signals section. The purpose of the demonstration and the continual reference to air raid shelters were undoubtedly meant to convince me that they were ready for any eventuality. I was frequently told that we in Europe were not doing enough to defend ourselves.

That was the end of this most interesting Manchurian trip. On our way back to Peking in the train I noticed some silver paper money held in place by a small sod of earth on top of a conical grave mound, which carried me back to the old China. Old customs and traditions die hard, particularly in country districts, and some members of the older generation still continue the practice. Ancestor worship forms no part of official government policy today, but the authorities are wise enough not to clamp down on those few members of the older generation who still practice it. Many of the grave mounds, which used to take up large areas of agricultural land, have been moved, and cremation is being encouraged by the Government.

Musing further I thought of the pros and cons of China old and new. The rising generation has been taught that old China before Liberation was chaotic, exploited by landlords and usurers, a prey to foreigners and incapable of standing on its own feet, all of which is true. The improvements have certainly been enormous—better and more general education, better medical services and hygiene, cleanliness, the emancipation of women, improved railways and better communications and roads, a higher and more equitable standard of living for all but the rich, a sense of purpose, a pride in the nation and above all a period of 30 years without any major civil war, if one discounts the excesses of the Cultural Revolution in which many thousands must have died. The price? Complete conformity and subjugation of the individual to the state and Communist Party. A by-product of the great material improvements and period of peace has been the huge increase in the population, one of the most difficult problems the Government has to face. Mao Ze Dong has sought literally to transform human nature, to make the Chinese people think solely of serving the people and not themselves, their own individuality to count for nothing except as members of a group. It remains to be seen how far such extremes of conformity and egalitarianism will last; Lenin's Russia has produced a privileged elite and a stratification of society which the Chinese abhor and call "revisionism". The longer you stay the more you become aware of the immense concentration of propaganda and the media on the top leadership and on Chairman Mao in particular.

Back in Peking I made a purchase at the Friendship Store, changed some Chinese yuan back into sterling and went off next morning to the airport with Wang to catch the Air France plane for Paris. On arrival I had to hand over my passport against a receipt, which was not returned until the last minute before boarding the plane—a sort of last minute hurdle you hope will be surmounted without difficulty.

All Chinese have a sound money sense, in spite of what Wang had told me about its irrelevance. The threat of a charge for any weight over and above the limit of 44 lb made some of the passengers pile large quantities of luggage into the passenger accommodation, over which there was little apparent control. There was a short stop at Karachi on the way back, and as I came out of the toilet at the airport, the hand of a tall man at the exit stretched out in front of me in search of a tip. Tipping is strictly illegal in China, which made me particularly notice the incident.

VIII
My Second Journey

THANKS to the experience gained before the first visit by air, I was better placed to plan a Siberian journey for the second. The Chinese Embassy in London produced visas for myself and my son quite quickly: I already knew about the necessity of booking a room in a Moscow hotel, before a transit visa for the Soviet Union could be issued, and reckoned that at least six weeks should be allowed for production of it. Just to make doubly sure, and keep a record of their visitors, the Russians make a photostat of your passport. We didn't reckon to go by train from East Berlin to Moscow, so there were no transit visas required for East Germany and Poland; the Mongolian visa was in the bag, as soon as the Soviet one materialised, which it did after six weeks, as expected.

We went in a Soviet Aeroflot plane from Heathrow to Moscow's Sheremetèvo airport. Here you get your first whiff of bureaucracy and the police state, as the place teems with soldiers, militia, passport checkers, customs men and Intourist officials. The Soviet Union is full of pen and pencil pushing bureaucrats, which makes it important for visitors to have absolutely correct documentation. The days of Gogol's *The Inspector General* are by no means over: they may indeed be in their infancy.

It was a Sunday night, and there was a general air of not much doing in the airport building, in spite of the many bureaucrats. "Six days shalt thou labour, and do all that thou hast to do" is supposedly the order of things in Christian countries in the West; the Soviet Union is supposedly Marxist and atheist, but one still has the feeling that the seventh day differs from the other six.

At last, more by accident than design, a bus was found to be going into the city, so we jumped into it. It is about 20 miles and it was pitch dark. All along the route are illuminated posters advertising various products, which seems an anomaly in a state supposedly controlling the means of production, distribution and exchange, thereby making competitive advertising unnecessary. One's first impression of the city, as it came into view, was one of unending blocks of flats, in which all the rooms appeared to be illuminated.

Our hotel was the "Rossia", an immense prestige establishment with 600 bedrooms overlooking the Moscow river. Four glass doors lead into the imposing foyer, but only one of them was open, the other three each carrying a notice marked "Bxod" or "Entrance", with arrows pointing to the open one. Here stood a uniformed official, who demanded to see your credentials, and pointed to the check-in desk. Here you lose your passport for the first time in the endless game of put and take, until you leave the country. When do we get them back? "Zabtra, zabtra— tomorrow, tomorrow" came the answer, and so we were rendered temporarily stateless for the first, but by no means the last, time. And so up to our rooms on the 11th floor, overlooking the Moscow river. It was 10.30 pm on a Sunday night, and the hotel quiet as the grave. You can get nothing of any kind—nothing stirs—everything is shut.

The tremendous, unceasing roar of Moscow's early morning traffic woke us up at 6 am; one might have been working in the production department of a great factory, so continuous and unbroken was the volume of sound. On the other side of the river a panel of neon lettering proclaims the slogan, "Communism is Soviet power plus the electrification of all countries" above a small generating station.

Food in the restaurant was very poor and, though the menu was enormous, the availability of the items on it was small. The waitresses, mostly large and buxom, did their best, but got little support from the kitchen.

Intourist, the Soviet travel organisation, had an office in the hotel and I eventually got our passports back in the late afternoon. We took a walk down to the very shabby British consulate, adjoining the Embassy, which had two smart, fur-hatted, armed sentries stationed at each entrance. Back in the hotel it was fascinating to watch the uniformed man at the entrance trying to check the credentials of those coming in and out. It was not clear whether he was trying to control foreigners coming in and going out, and stop Russians coming in—suffice it, that while he tried to grapple single-handed with a large party of American tourists coming in, two or three Russians, taking advantage of the melee by the door, stepped in quite unchecked. For a Russian to have foreign currency in his possession, without authority, is a heinous offence; the hotel is an ideal place in which to obtain it.

Red Square is the showpiece of the Soviet Empire, and is a must for visitors, Russian or foreign. It is an unforgettable sight, with the red crenellated walls round the Kremlin, the curious onion shaped domes of differing heights on the Basilius church, the ugly squat mausoleum containing the remains of Lenin, guarded by two smart sentries with fixed bayonets, the small white, named bricks in the Kremlin wall, behind which are the ashes of Russian heroes, and the paved surface of the great square itself, all combining to make a great impression on the visitor.

Not so the prestigious GUM Store, which has entrances off a side street, its wall facing on to the Red Square giving little indication that it is a commercial establishment. It dispenses every sort and kind of goods on two floors, including food, wine and vodka. We went in search of the food department, to get some extras for the Siberian train. The immense crowds at every food counter and cash desk defied description. No use offering money to make a purchase at the counter: you first had to determine the cost of what you wanted to buy, then get a cash ticket for the exact amount from a cashier in a small cage, and take it back to the counter in exchange for the goods. This meant that you not only had to know the price of everything you wanted to purchase, but had to queue twice for each transaction. Russians of both sexes tend to be large and bulky: the pushing and shoving was reminiscent of the scrum in a Rugby football match. Full marks to Moscow's housewives—the place is a hell on earth.

We set off on the evening of the second day in a taxi for the Yaroslav station. There to greet us at the station was a dapper little man from the Intourist office, who I knew had served as an interpreter in China. I asked him in my best Mandarin, "What is your Mandarin Chinese like these days?", whereupon he stuck both forefingers into his ears, and said, "We are not allowed to speak that language in Moscow."

The train, in its dark green livery, was already drawn up at the platform, Chinese attendants in their Mao caps standing outside each of the main passenger coaches: they were delighted to converse with a foreigner in their own tongue. Russians on the platform glared at them with open hostility—there was no disguising the fact of their mutual antipathy. Moscow-Ulan Bator-Peking read the indicator board on our coach—it must be one of the longest train journeys in the world. The railway is electrified the whole way to the Mongolian border; coaches are modern, built in East Germany, each with its own charcoal burning samovar and coal fired boiler. We set off at 8 p.m.

The Russian winter was over by the end of March, and the remains of the snow nearly melted away. Birch trees abounded and the scene was very reminiscent of the Dr. Zhivago film. The kolchos, or collective farms, with their small wooden houses and corrugated iron roofs, appeared from time to time, wretched look-ing dwellings, laid out at random with no apparent streets: piles of logs lay outside most of the houses, slush and mud everywhere.

Chinese car attendants outside the Siberian train

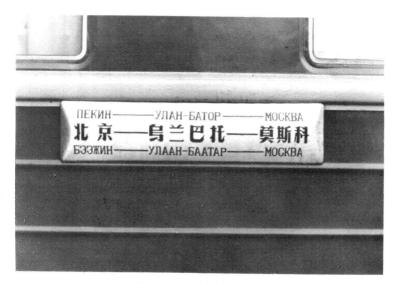

Siberian train indicator

The Russian mujik didn't seem to be getting much of a share of the great Russian Empire's goodies, apart from electrification and TV. Pylons and birch trees are my most lasting memories of the Siberian journey, both East and West of the Urals.

The line is double tracked, and goods trains of enormous length passed us from time to time going West. Quite a few of them were made up entirely of containers, probably taking Japanese exports from Vladivostock to Europe, thus bypassing the sea routes and greatly cutting down the time in transit. Timber and oil were the main commodities going West.

In our part of the train there were Swedes, Danes, Norwegians, Russians, Chinese and two Vietnamese, the last named facing another two and a half days in the train from Peking to Hanoi. Everyone, including the Chinese car attendants, piled into the small Russian dining car, where the food and beer was of poor quality, and many of the items on the menu unobtainable. Knives and forks, or chopsticks, as you pleased.

East of the Urals there is at first little change in the countryside. A line of small posts, carrying telephone wires and light electric cables, runs alongside the railway the whole way to Mongolia.

Breakfast with a diminutive Chinese from their embassy in Moscow—a deep, inscrutable individual with a marked Shanghai accent. As we looked out over the immense plain partly covered

A group of plate layers (mostly female) at a Siberian station

with snow, he remarked on it. "Yes," I said, "and there are practically no crops on it." The point was taken—the Chinese seldom fail to detect nuances of this kind.

I enquired of the Chinese attendant in our coach, whether he knew of any of his companions on the train, who might give me some lessons in Chinese, in return for some by me in English: he wasn't long in producing their top man, a keen student of English, who came to our compartment every day for a session. There are 22 Chinese staff on the train, and they do eight trips each way in a year.

The train stopped at Omsk, a large industrial city with over a million inhabitants, for 15 minutes (no stop is longer than this: there are 52 stops in all between Moscow and Peking.) A Russian soldier moved on a foreigner taking photographs of a group of giggling female platelayers. Behind some railings there is a ghastly plaster-of-paris statue of Lenin, which looks as if it might have been one of a general issue to all stations of a certain size. Each carriage has a minute charcoal burning samovar, and a larger coal burning boiler: little trucks run along the platform dispensing fuel for both.

The country is still quite flat. In a siding lies a collection of at least 30 rusting, jet black steam locomotives, relics of the pre-electric era. An odd diesel is to be seen on a branch line, but steam engines are a thing of the past.

The time change is already beginning to cause trouble: clocks are not officially advanced (by five hours) until the Mongolian border, but the staff took time by the forelock and closed the restaurant at 6 pm by their time, and only 4 pm by ours.

Novosibirsk is the next stop, again a large industrial town of over a million inhabitants on the imposing river Ob, one of the largest rivers in Siberia. You can break your journey here for a day or so, if you wish: as the name suggests, it is a modern city, with a pretentious new railway station, boasting raised platforms. This was Thursday—Monday's *Morning Star* was available at a kiosk for 20 kopecks (about 15 pence). On the platform opposite our carriage a burly man was standing, both hands stuck inside his coat, gazing into space. The Russians are particularly inept at disguising their stooges.

In the compartment next to ours were two North Vietnamese going back to Hanoi. They were obviously men of substance in the Communist world; no-one ever seemed to ask them for their passports or credentials. They were both small in stature, one speaking good Mandarin Chinese, and the other a little English.

As the clocks had not been changed, it was now broad daylight at 3 am, and a beautiful picture of pine and birch in deeper snow in a more undulating landscape met the eye. A fairly large kolchos then came into view, large patches of anything up to five hundred acres around it having been roughly cultivated. Then Krasnoyarsk on the mighty Yenisei river, boasting one of the biggest power-stations in the Soviet Union. What looked like hundreds of combine harvesters appeared to be lying out in the open on the side of the river; was it another of those failures to match demand with supply, which are common in the Soviet Union?

The Russian practice of sealing all carriage windows makes the compartments very fuggy and airless, the temperature being dictated by each coach attendant in charge of his own heating boiler. I couldn't make out whether the idea is to prevent passengers throwing things, or even themselves, out of the windows. News and music are broadcast in Chinese, but can be turned off in each compartment.

On Krasnoyarsk station my son was warned against taking a photograph by a pale, sinister looking individual in plain clothes. Two huge goods trains came thundering through the station taking timber and oil westwards, each of them well over 600 yards long. We had been warned that food on the train in Mongolia was very inadequate and tried to buy some butter from a small cabin-like shop on the station—none to be had.

The people had begun to look much more Mongolian in appearance, short and stocky with eyes set wider apart than the

Russians. The farther we got from Moscow, the greater appeared to be the volume of propaganda and exhortation—"Glory to Work", "Pay attention to Quality", "Celebrate the decision to revitalise the Communist Party". Perhaps the loyalty to Moscow grows less, the farther one gets away from it.

Other passengers were Sweden's leading female opera singer, a member of the Swedish Women's Federation party of seven going out to meet the equivalent federation in China, a Chinese importer of fancy goods from Birmingham with a British passport, on his way to the fair at Canton, a party of 21 Norwegians sponsored by the China/Norway Friendship Society, and a small, rather run-down little party of Danes under the same banner. To the Scandinavian peoples the Trans-Siberian Railway is the widely accepted means of travel to China.

The pine forests were beginning to get thinner: I travelled on this route 42 years ago and there has been a great deal of felling and little re-afforestation since then, scrub birch taking the place of the pines. All movement of timber on the rivers comes to a stop in the winter.

Now Irkutsk, one of Russia's earliest Siberian towns, situated not far from Lake Baikal, where there was a 10-minute stop. After leaving it, the train twisted and turned along the Southern shore of this vast lake, still frozen and snow covered, stretching away to the far horizon. Five thousand feet deep in places, it is frozen for about six months of the year. Men could be seen making holes in the thick ice with metal rods and catching fish quite close to the railway.

At the last two stops local women have been coming up to the restaurant car to buy apples and oranges from it. Untidiness everywhere—old boilers, piles of sleepers lying higgledy piggledy by the side of the railway, railway wheels and an old steam locomotive rusting away in a siding.

Ulan Ude, home of the Buriats, who closely resemble the Mongols, is where the Russian and Chinese trains diverge, to pass through Manchuria and Mongolia respectively. It has quite a modern appearance, with new blocks of flats, and a general look of orderliness about it. There was quite a number of uniformed militia on the platform and we were even able to buy some rolls from a shop on the platform.

As the train started running southwards towards Mongolia, you could begin to feel more warmth in the sun, until it reached Nauschke, the last town on the railway in Russia, where there was to be a scheduled stop of two hours and 50 minutes, for examination of passports and baggage, and exchange of any roubles back into foreign currency.

Shortly after the train had stopped, a tremendous five-star

female colonel, followed by a much smaller male attendant, also in uniform, boarded our coach and demanded our passports and details of any roubles we might have. The passports were taken away again, and we shuffled off to a tawdry office on the station platform, where roubles were exchanged for foreign currency, including the Mongol "tugrik", which should be avoided at all costs, as the notes are valueless outside Mongolia, and cannot be exchanged for any other currency. The passengers were then ordered back on to the train, and armed Russian soldiers were posted on each side of every coach.

The female colonel then re-appeared, gave us back our passports, and took a casual glance round our compartment, not deigning to search it—but wait, she had been extremely cunning, for two soldiers appeared and made a cursory search two minutes later, concentrating particularly, for some reason, on books and literature. The Chinese attendants were subjected to a much more rigorous search, which included lavatories, living quarters and storage cupboard; they looked nervous and subdued while this was going on. The train could obviously be the means of passing information to Peking.

Three and a half hours later we were still sitting in Nauschke, as the Mongols hadn't produced a locomotive: electrification finishes here and from now on the train is pulled by a diesel. The time had changed, and we didn't get away from Nauschke until 1.30 am. The first Mongolian town of Such Bator is only 20 miles away, where another search and passport check takes place. We decided to sleep in spite of this.

At Such Bator, about an hour later, we were woken up by two uniformed Mongolian officers, who took our passports; another man following them handed out a form made out in Russian; in a few minutes he came back again and said, "Peking?" to which we answered, "Yes", whereupon he promptly took the form away again, uncompleted.

The next morning we reached Ulan Bator (formerly Urga), the capital of Mongolia. The station and central part of the town have been entirely rebuilt, with broad streets and imposing blocks of modern flats. The Russians must have contributed heavily to the rebuilding of the city, as the resources of Mongolia, three times the size of France and with a population of only one and a half million, must be scanty.

Great activity on the station itself—older Mongolian men wearing brown kaftan-like coats, with bright yellow sashes, their bow legs in soft boots, men trained to the saddle like their great predecessor, Genghis Khan; small children still wearing their fur hats with the flaps down over their ears (it is a chill wind here at 5,000 feet), a few Mongolian soldiers in fur caps looking like

Children at a small Siberian station

their Russian counterparts, while standing behind the closed windows of the main station building were a number of Russian soldiers gazing at the train. Not much doubt about who calls the tune here. Photography is forbidden; the Mongols (or their masters) are very allergic to it.

The single tracked Trans-Mongolian Railway was built in the 1950s to cut down the transit time on the old Trans-Siberian route across Manchuria, which takes 24 hours longer. Miles of utterly flat, parched, brown steppe are on each side of the railway, with here and there an isolated collective farm, a few cattle and horses, and an odd camel. Suddenly a man or woman, standing beside a saddled pony quite close to the railway, and holding aloft a short pole headed by a yellow, circular disc, came into view—for all the world like a lollipop man shepherding children across a street coming out from school. The purpose is not clear, unless it replaces a signalling system to prevent a head-on collision, as the single track has many curves and loops and few passing places. We passed a train of Russian tanks, complete with crews, lying in a siding.

The train now had a Mongolian restaurant car, in which the food was poor and the prices high. There was inflation in Mongolia, and their "tugrik" currency was valueless outside their own country. There are about 8,000 overseas Chinese living in Ulan Bator, who come back from China laden with goods, as the Mongolian prices are so high.

The train stopped at Choyren, about 130 miles on from Ulan Bator. It looked like a military communications centre, with barracks, wireless aerials and air raid shelters near the railway. We passed another trainload of Russian tanks with crews. By about 1.30 am we had covered the 400-odd miles from Ulan Bator, and reached the Mongolian border town of Dzamyn Uud.

I was half asleep in the bottom bunk of our two berth compartment, when there was a knock on the door, which opened quietly. Automatically I reached for my passport for the third time in two nights, and found myself handing it to a small gentleman in short white coat and side cap, reminiscent of the then Indian Premier, Mr. Desai. He immediately handed the passport back again. I wondered if I had been selected for treatment in one of those dreaded Russian mental institutions. Nothing so dramatic—his job was to vaccinate anyone unable to produce a certificate of vaccination. Next came two uniformed Mongolians on the hunt for films and subversive literature. They made everyone open their cameras, thus exposing the film (if any). The Norwegians lost seven films: fortunately we had been forewarned.

On again to Erhlien, the first town on the railway in China, which we reached at about 5.40 am. A small, neat station with its name in blue neon lettering, and an atmosphere of calm after the feeling of tension in Mongolia. The wheels of the train had to be changed here to fit the different gauge of the Chinese railway system.

Three representatives of the China Travel Service were on the station to greet us, and we had an excellent meal of prawns and rice on the new restaurant car, which had not yet been hooked up to the train. The fourth lot of formalities inside 48 hours were soon completed—all of them had been late at night or in the early hours of the morning.

After travelling for some time through uncultivated, poor-looking country, the familiar type of Chinese countryside begins to appear again, with intensively cultivated small plots. This is Inner Mongolia, part of China, into which the Chinese have pushed from further south with their intensive methods of cultivation: an odd brick kiln could be seen, a few electric pylons, an odd tractor and a vehicle or two—but horse carts predominated on any of the roads to be seen. Glass is beginning to replace the transparent rice paper in the windows of houses. Production teams of around 20 people have taken the place of men working in twos and threes in the old China.

The train stopped more frequently in China—in quick succession at Datong, Xuanhua and Xhangjiakau, all places which

I knew of old. Then, in the distance, the outlines of the Great Wall could be seen, going up hill and down dale, for all the world like some gigantic snake. At Nankou, near which the train travelled underneath the wall, it eventually debouched on to the plain of North China, a hive of agricultural activity, with more and more vegetables being grown, as it drew nearer to Peking.

We had been travelling for five days and 15 hours, when we eventually drew into Peking's main station. Apart from the Russian train via Manchuria, which takes 24 hours longer, this must be the longest single train journey in the world in one set of coaches. There waiting on the platform was none other than my old friend Wang from the previous visit.

The new marble floored Peking station, with its moving staircase, is enormous, with vast crowds milling about both inside and outside it—our first contact with the mass of the 900 million people in this country, with an area almost exactly the same as the United States, and over four times its population.

IX
Peking, Nanking, Yangzhou and Wuxi, 1977

Zhu De, Zhou En-Lai and Mao Ze Dong

I MUST be careful not to surfeit the reader with too much of Peking; I had come for a second visit mainly to introduce my son, who had never previously been in China, to some of the glories of the capital and its surrounding areas.

Since the 1974 visit Mao Ze Dong had died in 1976, as had the other two chief architects in the building of the new Republic, Zhou En Lai and Zhu De. The construction of the massive memorial to Mao on the Tian An Men Square was proceeding apace; the Gang of Four had been exposed and arrested, thus preventing what might quite easily have become a civil war between the followers of Mao's widow Jiang Qing and those of the newly appointed leader Hua Guo Feng. Jiang Qing had been a highly unpopular figure with the Chinese public and her arrest was generally greeted with a sigh of relief as well as a good omen for the future of the new leader. It was too soon after Mao's death for the later far reaching changes to become apparent, though the number of foreign tourists and delegations of all kinds had visibly increased.

We visited a rather progressive commune just outside Peking called Evergreen, with a population of 46,000 and, which specialised in the production of fruit, vegetables, ducks and pigs for the capital—so much so, that it grew insufficient grain for its own members which had to be augmented by purchases from the state.

The official who gave us particulars was on the staff of the commune and a member of the Communist Party. He told us that the committee responsible for the commune had 31 members, of which 14 were vice-chairmen; election of committee members, including that of the chairman, took place every three years, after discussion and debate lasting over 10 days. A small standing committee was responsible for the day to day running of affairs. The commune staff numbered 120, of which 70 were on a salary basis and paid by the state and 50 employed by the commune and paid by work points. All staff members had to do manual work for a specified period, which appeared to be 120 days in the year.

Of particular interest was a class in one of the primary schools making use of pin yin, or phonetics, as an aid to the pronunciation of the spoken equivalents of the Chinese characters they were learning to write. This was apparently not the first stage in the adoption of pin yin for general use, but merely an experiment to accelerate the learning of the spoken word. One monosyllable in Mandarin can be represented by anything up to 50 different characters; the application of phonetics side by side with the characters or pictographs makes the equivalent sounds easier to understand and memorise. Anything that can speed up the learning of the language, which takes up an inordinate amount of teaching time, is to be welcomed.

Number Five middle school, situated in the centre of the city, had senior and junior sections totalling 2,450 pupils. It was near a main road and such was the noise of traffic and hooting that the tape recording I took was nearly drowned out. Junior pupils who previously left at the age of 12 were now leaving at 10; methods of teaching and examining had been drastically changed. It was said that too much attention had been paid to learning by heart and to repetition, that theory had been divorced from practice and that children had been too spoon-fed; they were now being given problems to solve themselves. Under the old examination system teachers had been inclined to regard their pupils as enemies to be outwitted by asking them difficult questions. Now the subjects for examinations were not published in advance and methods were more open in character.

During the Cultural Revolution Mr. Wang, who accompanied us round the school, had been criticised by his pupils as a revisionist. At first he could not accept the criticisms aimed at him—he had used the systems criticised for many years to his own satisfaction. Only by studying the Thoughts of Mao had he come to appreciate the wisdom of the new methods employed.

I asked how young people found their jobs later in life. Were they simply directed or did they have any say in their future careers? One of the young teachers in the school had been sent out to a commune at age 19 and had worked there for six years. More teachers were required in Peking and the commune where she worked had been informed of this; the peasants and the headquarters of the commune had agreed to her applying for the job, which she had got, the same system applying for those who wished to be considered for a university. This was the only school I had visited where Russian, and not English, was being taught as the first foreign language. I don't think this had any political significance. During the honeymoon period from 1950 to 1960 there had been at least 50,000 Sino-Soviet friendly societies and Russian had been the first foreign language in the schools. The sudden change in policy and departure of the Russians, coupled with the decision to make English the first foreign language, found them woefully short of English teachers.

Before we set out on our next journey I asked Wang if he was going to see his wife and daughter before we left. He said he wasn't and appeared entirely disinterested.

Nanking, the Southern capital, as opposed to Peking, the Northern capital, was our next destination and we went by train. Chiang K'ai Shek, when in power, had Nanking as his capital, but it was brought back to Peking by Mao. As we got further South the landscape began to change as did the crops, rice and the paddy fields becoming much more in evidence. Grave mounds were everywhere to be seen, some with paper money on them put there by relatives. Country people are traditionally more conservative than those in the towns and we got the impression that the idea of cremation had not so thoroughly permeated the country districts. At the end of the journey we crossed the Yangtse on the massive new bridge completed in 1968, an imposing construction carrying both road and rail.

On our way out to the hotel we visited the Memorial to the Heroes of the Revolution at Yu Hua Tai, situated near the old

Yu Hua Tai memorial at Nanking

execution ground where many Communist followers had been shot by Chiang K'ai Shek's Kuomintang during the years of revolution. A small building was devoted mainly to a display of photographs of those who had been executed, with biographical notes; outside was a memorial in stone on which many floral paper wreaths had been placed. It was a grim and gruesome place to visit after a long and tiring rail journey.

Nanking is very spread out and has a large city wall which still appears to be intact. Not far outside the city, at Zhongshan, there is a rather squat and unattractive mausoleum containing the remains of Sun Yat Sen, whom one might describe as the doyen of Chinese revolutionaries; it lies on a hillside, is approached by a long very wide flight of stone steps and is a place of pilgrimage. Sun Yat Sen died in Peking in 1925 and I well remember seeing the special train carrying his coffin from there to Nanking in 1929.

Our only other visit in Nanking was to a teacher training college, which had previously been a training centre for American missionaries. The introductory proceedings were rather dull and heavily interlarded with politics. Should the students be of bourgeois or worker/peasant origin? Should they be trained to be both "red" and "expert"? There were usually 50 in classes in Kiangsu province middle schools. We must have consumed a great deal of tea, as my tape recording of the interview continually gives the familiar sucking noise of tea being imbibed. It is considered right and proper in China to drink and eat quite noisily as a proof that you are enjoying what is put before you. The students, most of them from the local province of Jiangsu, were being trained as teachers in middle schools; about 40 per cent of them were girls and they were likely to stay in their own province. We visited one or two classes, in one of which the students asked my son, who is an actor, to give them a rendering in English. He chose a passage by Shylock in the *Merchant of Venice* which had a rapturous reception from the students who had obviously had little experience of English spoken as it should be.

Yangzhou is a sizeable town north of the Yangtse about 80 kilometres northeast of Nanking. Going by road you cross the river on the new bridge, travelling above the railway. We had a brief stop in a reception room at the railway level, where a young woman gave details of the bridge, including some rhetoric about the Gang of Four. A long goods train, pulled by a steam engine, came thundering past as we were there. It is said that locomotives and rolling stock on the Chinese railways are turned round quicker than in any other country in the world.

Having hooted about half way to Yangzhou, we stopped at

Sun Yat Sen memorial at Zhongshan

Special train carrying Sun's coffin in 1929

a state farm quite close to the road, where we had a warm welcome and where there was a notable absence of the political topics usually aired on such occasions. The farm was growing apples, peaches, pears and plums on a fairly large scale on rather poor land. State farms are set up by the government in areas requiring considerable capital outlay; workers are paid a fixed wage, and not by the work points system as in the communes. In north Manchuria particularly, where there is virgin land, state farms have been developed for growing grain crops on a large scale where combine harvesters can be used.

Yangzhou has been the centre of lacquer production since the 17th century. At the time of Liberation there were three small workshops employing 20 people; production has now been centralised in one factory employing 700 workers. Centralisation has increased the number of designs and promoted research. The black or red lacquer is inlaid with many different materials such as jade, mother-of-pearl, ivory, coral and many others. Much of the production of furniture, screens and other items is exported.

Asked about labour the chairman of the revolutionary committee said there were more applicants for jobs than they could take, in spite of the very low rates of pay from a minimum of 40 to a maximum of 80 yuan per month (about £13 to £26). For beginners there was a three year apprenticeship, starting with drawing, before the operation of any machines. Had machines worsened quality? No, the reverse was true; both quality and the number of designs had improved. Though I saw no "da zi bao" hanging up in the factory, I was assured that criticisms were welcomed at any time. It was again noticeable that those in charge were in the 30 to 40 age group. A well run factory, but as usual very noisy.

Judging by the large crowds who followed and gazed at us, as if we were from another planet, there cannot have been many foreign visitors in Yangzhou. We were going to a miniature lake, based on the famous Western Lake at Hangzhou, which was full of weeds and not well cared for, though I was told that there were supposed to be some 200 people looking after it; one got the impression that there was a good deal of hidden unemployment in the town.

Then in the afternoon on to Guazhou, near a point where the Grand Canal, built some 1500 years ago, and linking the Yangtse with the Yellow river in Shandong province, joins the Yangtse. Not far from the canal a pumping station had been built to serve the double purpose of allowing small vessels through a lock and controlling the water level of some thirty three thousand acres of land, which had previously suffered from extremes of drought

Goods train crossing rail and road bridge

A Manchurian state farm for growing grain

and flood. The Grand Canal itself which had narrowed, become silted up and was badly neglected during the civil war era, has been widened and straightened; near Guazhou a new lock has been built with a basin 250 metres in length, capable of taking vessels of up to 4,000 tons. Further up the canal seven other new locks have been built.

As we hooted our way back to Peking, agricultural work was in full swing in the well tended fields, polythene being much in evidence as a cover on the beds of young rice. The road was full of lorries, walking tractors and bicycles but there were few horse drawn vehicles to be seen.

Wuxi, our next stop, is a city of 650,000 population situated close to the Taihu lake, one of the largest inland lakes in the country. Our hotel looked out over it and it was fascinating to see the small sailing vessels knifing their way out to the fishing grounds, while in front of the hotel there was a massive display of peach blossom in full bloom—truly a wonderful setting. The hotel itself was rather austere internally, with bare, unadorned passages and a long row of identical arm chairs, all with their anti-macassars, drawn up against the wall of the foyer. A stand carrying numerous copies of the *Peking Review* in every conceivable language attracted little interest. Only the dining room was colourful with pictures on the walls and six great buckets of rice on the floor, from which the guests could help themselves and refill their plates. There was the usual Friendship shop, where I made the terrible mistake of asking for a box of matches known to me by their old name of "yang huo" or "foreign fire". Prestige had dictated their renaming as "huo chai" or "fire sticks" to remove the foreign taint.

A factory making figurines was our first visiting point. As we went round it, I noticed charts which appeared to be showing production figures. I asked what they were and was told, "Jiang Qing limited the number of designs we could use on our figurines; some of them indeed had to be scrapped, because they were considered not to be sufficiently revolutionary, so now that she is out of the way, we are making up for lost time and increasing production." My son asked the factory manager, "If you have two employees doing the same sort of work and one is noticeably better at it than the other, how do you improve the lot of the better performer?" The answer after a long delay was that they could not come to a decision on their own in a matter of this kind, as wages were strictly controlled by the government.

The Grand Canal or a branch of it passes through the city of Wuxi and there was an unending line of boats on it, with powered barges pulling anything up to 10 tows; endless crowds

Jade carving with mechanical aid

and the usual interminable hooting of car horns completed the picture.

In the evening there was a very well-acted performance by children from primary and middle schools from a local commune in the hotel theatre, somewhat marred by Japanese members of the audience constantly clicking their cameras with flashlight and even walking right up to the edge of the stage to do so. The famous lion dance was very professionally done.

Next day we were at a plant making diesel engines for pumps and marine propulsion in fishing vessels, some of those for the latter being up to 1,350 horse power. In one department where the organisation and flow of work seemed most haphazard I ventured to ask who was the foreman in charge, a question which provoked gales of laughter from my companions. "Foreman" is apparently a bad word, conjuring up in the Chinese mind memories of brutal men in Japanese factories urging on Chinese workers to ever increasing production; it also smacks of "commandism", an undesirable trait in a people who love to debate and argue before reaching a consensus of opinion and a final decision. Workers in factories, theoretically at least, elect their own leaders from the managing director downwards. In welfare terms this factory was extremely well provided for—it had a canteen, a library, an art room and medical and dental facilities, including X-ray, provided by a welfare grant from the central government based on 11 per cent of the total wage bill. Many of the firm's workers were accommodated in the firm's newly built flats.

I was prompted at this point to try and make a comparison between Chinese industry and that in Britain. A working week of 48 hours compared with one of 40, or sometimes less, no pay for overtime against double or triple time in Britain, wage rates of say the equivalent of £3 to £9 per week against £60 to say £120 per week, holidays on national days totalling 11 per year against three to four weeks with six to eight statutory holidays thrown in, a working week of six days against five. Wages in eight grades are controlled nationally, the trade unions being organs of government and in no way involved with wage negotiations. The cost of living is of course far lower than with us; inflation is minimal, all prices being government controlled, and there is no tax on earned income, so that comparisons between the rewards of labour are difficult.

Silk is an important industry in the Wuxi area and it was fascinating to visit a silk filature employing 600 people, mostly women, which had been in existence before Liberation. Hairraising stories were told of the employment of child labour, of the working of a 14-hour day and of certain times of the year when workers never caught a glimpse of the sun on work days. Since Liberation production had risen eight fold, while the removal of the Gang of Four had resulted in a 15 per cent increase in production. In 1976 China had lost the three main architects of the new republic in the shape of Mao Ze Dong, Zhou En Lai and Zhu De. It was logical to assume that, if joy increased production, sorrow might retard it, so I asked if production had been adversely affected in 1976, to which no answer was given. Perhaps the 15 per cent increase was simply a "façon de parler" to underline the dislike of the Gang of Four; in any case exactitude in quoting figures is not one of China's strong points.

As in so many other branches of industry the culture of silk worms before Liberation had been a cottage industry; more recently the mulberry leaves were being brought in to a central point to feed the caterpillars, which make cocoons and spin the silk round them. Inside the cocoons are larvae, some of which are set aside for reproduction; the remainder, after being boiled to extract gum, then have their silk unwound on machines and spun into silk thread, 10 cocoons being used for each silken thread. Great skill is required to correct any breaks in the thread and on a new spinning machine developed in the filature one woman is able to supervise six spinning operations simultaneously. The finished article undergoes seven rigid quality

Women picking silk cocoons

controls. Italy appears to be the chief competitor in this field. This was an efficient, well organised production unit.

In spite of regimentation the Chinese still manage to retain their individuality and will never lose it. Many little incidents in and around Wuxi stand out in my mind. We came round a corner in the car, and here was an old man walking along in the middle of the road behind a party of at least a hundred fully grown white ducks, using a long bamboo pole to guide them and keep them in order. On another occasion a local sportsman passed us on a bicycle, gun slung over his shoulder and small dog safely strapped to the carrier behind. Courtesy and good manners, of which we see too little in the West, are inbred in most Chinese. In the mornings the weather forecast was studied and umbrellas were always placed in the car if rain was threatening. Suddenly outside a village on a main road we came on a party of peasants waving red flags to celebrate the publishing of the fifth volume of the *Thoughts of Chairman Mao*. Surprises too. We went down to a pier giving on to the Taihu lake and suddenly found ourselves on a magnificent, powered, pavilion-like boat, big enough to take at least 20 people, on which we went for a spin on the lake among the fishing boats. The foundations were being built for a new hotel to accommodate the rapidly rising flood of tourists. For the first time I saw an army barracks where many of the soldiers were out tending the land; every Chinese has an attachment to the land. It is no bad thing for soldiers to be self sufficient for food, particularly in the far northern frontier districts where communications, except by air, may be difficult. The patched clothing of the peasants was noticeable, many of them looking like harlequins, for cloth is rationed.

On an island on the lake, close inshore, is the Wuxi Taihu Workers Sanatorium, completed in 1952, with 300 sick beds and a staff of 120. It is there for the rehabilitation of industrial workers suffering from non-infectious complaints, like chest and gastric trouble, arthritis, eye trouble, respiratory complaints, neuralgia and so forth. Entrance is by recommendation by the health authorities or factory committee, the average length of stay being three months, during which the inmates get their full rate of pay and extra rations. There are no medical fees. Physical exercise in the beautiful surroundings is encouraged; indoors there is chess and shadow boxing, a TV room, study of Marxism and the Thoughts of Mao and occasional films.

After we had gone the rounds and had gathered for question time, I remarked at one point, referring to the great preponderance of young school age children in Wuxi, that we also had an imbalance between the age groups; in our case however it was the growing preponderance of the older age groups, so much so, I added in a rash moment, that suggestions had been made in some quarters that we should practise euthanasia. I could almost sense those present literally pricking up their ears with curiosity, as they enquired, "And what is that?" I explained to them that in certain cases of terminal, incurable disease it had been suggested that patients should be allowed quietly to pass away, and no longer be kept alive. The spry young Communist "ganbu" immediately said, "Oh, Chairman Mao would never have allowed a thing like that to happen". It was obvious to me that word would get around that the British take no steps to look after their old people when they are ill, and simply let them die for want of care and attention. I added quickly that euthanasia was not being practised, that it had merely been suggested and publicised by some and would they please not report to their next branch meeting that "the British take no care of their old people when they are ill and simply let them die". It was an object lesson in not introducing contentious subjects to a Communist audience unaccustomed to the free exchange of opinions in our democratic society, and only too willing to make capital out of them for propaganda purposes.

At these sessions questions came almost invariably from the

visitors and I asked if no-one had a question to put to me. A young man then asked me, if it was true that young people who get married in the West immediately set up a home of their own. "Generally speaking they do" I replied "unless they have been unable to find a suitable house, in which case they may temporarily live with their in-laws, but this is the exception rather than the rule". Whether due to tradition or a shortage of houses, it is customary for young marrieds in China to live with their in-laws, at least in the early stages of their married life.

X
Suzhou, Hangzhou and Shanghai, 1977

THERE were large crowds waiting for the train to Suzhou, orderly groups being interspaced at intervals exactly the same as those between the carriage doors. Queueing for buses or trains or in shops is endemic in China; queues are accepted as a normal part of life and there is no jostling or pushing to get a better place. We as foreigners were privileged to enter a second class coach, which we had all to ourselves, any Chinese passengers having been turned out.

Suzhou, mentioned by Marco Polo in his writings, is a beautiful and typically Chinese city of half a million people with tree-lined streets and many gardens developed by wealthy residents before Liberation. There were 500 wealthy landlords and capitalists in the city at that time.

In the afternoon we went off to another commune quite close to the Taihu lake, where one of the many vice chairmen received us. It had a population of about 47,000 (curious how many communes seem to have populations of about that size) and a wide variety of activities, which illustrated how enterprise in a commune away from pure agriculture can flourish to its undoubted advantage. Food production consisted of fish from 3,000 acres of ponds fed from the lake, tea, fruit and some food grains for their own consumption; prominent amongst the fruit crop was the loquat, a fruit I had never seen before, described in the dictionary as "rush orange"; two small factories processed tea and dried fruit; the foundations had also been laid for a hotel. The profit motive was strongly in evidence, and figures were given to show how the incomes of the commune members had increased; in one year half a million yuan (about £165,000) had been deposited in the bank at an interest rate of 2.7 per cent on an annual basis and 1.18 per cent for short term saving. Members liked to save up for family occasions like births and weddings or to buy furniture, a sewing machine or a bicycle. In the middle school pin yin was being extensively used; nearly a third of teaching time was being devoted to the Chinese and English languages. In constructive hand work the girls were sewing and embroidering, the boys carving, making small harmoniums and working with electronics.

I asked the vice chairman about the nationwide destruction of sparrows which had been ordered some years previously. He admitted that it had been a great mistake and had greatly increased the number of pests. "Do you follow developments in the model commune at Dazhai?" I asked. He said they had followed the great pioneering achievements there and were interested in the new experimental developments now being carried out, which he described. Houses of two storeys were being built, with living accommodation upstairs, and feeding and recreational activities downstairs. The small production teams were being abolished and the brigades being made the smallest organisational unit. Private family plots were being done away with in favour of larger communal plots for all those living in one housing compound. All these experiments, if adopted, would of course still further reduce the individual's range of action and merge him or her more completely in a group.

At one point I tried out a carrying pole with filled buckets of water, one at each end of the pole. In order to keep the load perfectly steady, you have to cultivate a brisk walk with very short steps, similar to those you see used by competition walkers. It is a favourite means of carrying goods, especially in Central and South China where the many waterways restrict road communications.

The making of fans has been an industry in Suzhou for over 2,000 years. Fan makers working individually in a cottage industry had numbered 40; there was now a factory employing over 500 and turning out over two million fans per year. Fans are of many types—court fans, bamboo, ivory, peacock feather and sandalwood, the natural aroma from which never fades. Amongst the 300 different designs and motifs, some were traditional and some depicting developments in industry such as electricity, railways, coal mining and steel making, and in agriculture irrigation pumps and tractors. One design depicted the chain bridge over the Da Tu river in Western China, the capture of which by Mao's forces in the civil war against Chiang Kai Shek was one of the epics of the Long March in 1934/5.

The Embroidery Institute was the next port of call, where it was again the same story of individual workers being brought together in the interest of more research, the exchange of ideas, a bigger range of designs and greater production. There was a designing studio, one for painting and the actual embroidery workshops. The number of different stitches used, they said, had been increased from 12 to 40 and double-sided embroidery had been introduced. As in the case of fans there were two categories of design, ancient and modern, in the latter

The author with two interpreters on an island in West Lake, Hangzhou

of which the new Nanking bridge was prominent. There was also a huge tapestry depicting the Great Wall, which I judged to be very ugly. Quite a lot of the work seemed to be for public bodies, exhibitions and official functions. I had often heard of blindness amongst embroiderers in the old China, due to the intense concentration required for the work in often poor lighting conditions, and enquired what steps were taken to avoid this. They said the girls worked an eight hour day with breaks every two hours for eye exercises; there was no evening work. The building was new and the lighting conditions excellent. Apprentices were trained in all three branches of the art.

We had an early start to catch the train for Hangzhou, which went via Shanghai. As we sat in the station waiting room, embellished by a large portrait of Chairman Mao, one of his poems and several beautiful azaleas in full bloom, our interpreter broached the everlasting subject of the Gang of Four, which he said had done particular harm to the railway system, now restored to normal working. Unfortunately for him the train arrived a good half hour late! As Mao gazed down at us from the wall of the waiting room, one was tempted to paraphrase Churchill's famous eulogy of the Royal Air Force in the Battle of Britain by saying, "Never in the field of human endeavour have so many been subject to so few".

The Hangzhou hotel faced the large West Lake which is right in the city and renowned throughout China for its beauty. Unusually, a sentry with rifle and fixed bayonet was mooching up and down outside the hotel, for what reason I never gathered. Whatever their fighting qualities may have been in the war against the Japanese, Chinese soldiers have never impressed me by their turnout and military bearing.

We took a boat trip to the island of "The Three Pools Mirroring the Moon", where visitors were feeding carp and goldfish with biscuit crumbs from a small bridge over a slow running stream, and others posing their families and children for photographs. Unlike our people who frequently take pictures of scenery, views, buildings or flowers in bloom, the Chinese seem to concentrate entirely on people.

The Plum Village brigade of the West Lake's People's Commune was an interesting place, though quite small with only 1,100 people in 250 households, mostly employed in the picking and drying of tea. Tea bushes covered about 190 acres and trees another 600—the soil was poor. The land had previously belonged to three landlords who had hired out the inhabitants to work for them. We were greeted in the house of one of them, now the brigade's headquarters, by a woman vice-chairman.

Drying tea

A tea-picking machine

After she had given us the usual particulars of the steady
increases in tea production and the amount of savings banked
by the commune members, I asked if the meeting was being
held in the house of one of the landlords. "Yes indeed" she
replied "and I was here when all three of them were subjected
to public criticism at the time of Liberation. One of them was
actually persecuted (from which I deduced he had been killed;)
he had been guilty of ruthlessly exploiting the peasants". "And
what happened to the other two?" I asked. "Both of them lost
their properties and their political rights, and were put to work
in the production teams at the same rate of pay as the other
workers. Every year the peasants made an assessment of their
work and attitudes; one of them is a reformed character, and
has since been rehabilitated and had his political rights restored;
the other, unable to forget his lost paradise, has committed
sabotage, in that he deliberately drowned one of the brigade's
piglets and purposely left two or three stones out of a terrace
wall which was being built, so that after a heavy rainfall water
came rushing through the gap to the terrace below, thus causing
great damage to it. He is still subject to constant supervision
by the peasants and an annual appraisal of his work.

My son asked her if she had heard of or seen the new tea

picking machine in use in some parts of the country. She said they had seen it, but it was of no use to them, as their tea bushes were too close together and their tea of such high quality that it had to be picked by hand. "Had they been able to use it, would it have caused some unemployment in the brigade? he asked. "On the contrary" she replied "we are short of labour and want, not only to extend the area under cultivation, but also to diversify into other forms of employment".

Asked about production and finance arrangements in the brigade, she said that production target figures were sent down annually by the commune to the brigade, which were then discussed and amended up or down by the production teams if necessary, until agreement was reached on settled target figures. The revenue produced from their sale of tea to the state, less a small percentage deduction for tax, was used partly to pay for the work points earned by members of the production teams, partly as a credit to public welfare funds for services in the brigade area and partly as a credit to a capital accumulating fund, out of which the cost of capital items, such as tractors, vehicles, tools and agricultural equipment was met. The value of the work points was dependent partly on the amount earned from the crop of tea and partly on the value of the amounts allocated to the special funds, which was a matter for discussion within the brigade itself. Some food grains had to be bought in, as their land was unsuited to growing them.

Owing to indisposition I was unable to visit a factory making brocades, a traditional industry in Hangzhou; the product is bright and colourful and I bought several cushion covers made of it. The factory, like so many others, was reported to be very noisy.

That evening at dinner in the hotel restaurant a small party of foreigners came in, closely shepherded by three or four Chinese, and disappeared into a side room. I remarked to my son, "I think those people are British, don't you?" "Yes— I agree" and no more was said.

Finally to Shanghai by train, where the party we had seen the previous evening were in the same coach—about 10 of them in all. "I think they are schoolmasters" I whispered to my son. "That man over there doing all the talking looks like a typical public school master and the domineering lady like the head mistress of a girls school". Nothing more was said until we boarded the plane for home, of which more anon.

Shanghai is by far the biggest city in China with a population of well over 10 million. Originally a walled town, it was developed by foreigners from its occupation in 1843, first as a port for imports and exports and subsequently as the main industrial centre of the country, which it still is. That part of it formerly occupied by foreigners in the International and French settlements is entirely Western in appearance in contrast to the essentially Chinese quarters surrounding them. During the foreign occupation Shanghai was well known for its night life and for the bar in the International Club, reputed to be the longest in the world.

We were housed in what used to be the prestigious Victor Sassoon hotel, now renamed the He Ping, fronting on to the Huangpu river, a tributary of the Yangtse. Foreign warships used to lie off in the river quite close to the hotel. The hooting of steamers was now added to the hooting of motor horns; to add still further to the noise a fearful explosion of fireworks and crackers suddenly erupted just outside the hotel. Celebrating the publication of the fifth volume of Mao's Thoughts? A visit to Shanghai by the new Chairman Hua Guo Feng? Not a bit of it. Chairman Hua was making a speech on the Four Modernisations at the oil producing centre at Daqing in North Manchuria and this was to draw the attention of the citizens to it. In the restaurant all the furniture, except that actually in use was piled up in a corner, for this was national spring cleaning week in all the hotels, as we had already noticed in Hangzhou.

The large well laid out industrial exhibition hall in the city is designed to show the progress of engineering. Huge generators were on show as well as vehicles and, of special interest, prototypes of two machines for planting and harvesting rice, two of the most back breaking jobs in the country. There was an unusual mechanical exhibit showing model members of each of the minority races, in their appropriate national dress, moving round inside a large showcase singing their national songs.

Pengbu on the outskirts of Shanghai is a good example of a newly developed, tightly organised urban commune, to which we were introduced by a woman vice-chairman of the commune's central committee, obviously a very dedicated Communist. "Conditions in the old foreign dominated Shanghai had been very bad" she said, "with low pay, long hours, and bad housing conditions. Pengbu was a new and developing workers residential area with a population of 20,000 in 5,000 households. It was a young population, with 7,000 of the total population being of school age. Men and women of working age were employed in nearby industries; those who had retired and were fit to work and women without factory employment were all employed in the commune. A small number of women were left in the blocks of flats to look after people who were sick or for some reason unable to work. The death of Chairman Mao had been a great tragedy for China; some of the residents had stopped eating for days in their grief". We saw

166

later two wooden huts where women were assembling shoes and putting simple toys together, most of the work apparently being sub-contracted by manufacturers. Both shops were very overcrowded and the conditions would not have been tolerated by workers in the West. The organisation of the residents appeared to be total, with no-one unemployed—I should not have liked to live there.

The area was self contained as to hospitals and schools, with a kindergarten for 600 children. Savings in the Peoples Bank had reached two million yuan (nearly £700,000). Houses were repaired free; rents were 20 cents per square metre per month. There was a bank, a post office, a public dining hall, a vegetable market and 24 shops, shortly to be increased in number. The whole area was run by an elected central committee of 11, with five sub-committees in different residential areas.

Traffic on the streets was heavy and they were already full of people by the time we set off for the main food market in Shanghai, due to open at 6 a.m. Quite young boys were trying to control the traffic; organised parties of children were moving about; some of the older generation were already practising their Tai Ji Tuan, a form of shadow boxing, on the Bund. The headquarters of the Shanghai Communist Party are now established in the magnificent building on the Bund, which used to be the head office of the Hongkong and Shanghai Bank; as we passed it, a small open truck, with several men in the back and two rows of red flags fluttering in the breeze, drew up, and its passengers disappeared into the building. I enquired what it was all about and was told that it was a delegation from some local factory come to report some outstanding production figures.

The food market itself was teeming with people buying vegetables, meat, fish, fowls, ducks and eggs, some of the produce being ready prepared for cooking. At a small booth a man was taking complaints of sharp practice, short weight, poor quality and so forth. Life is highly competitive in a society not all that far above the bread line. The progress made in the equitable distribution of what is available has been remarkable; I saw no sign anywhere of a beggar or of malnutrition.

The Children's Palace, once the home of a wealthy Parsee merchant said to have made a fortune out of opium, is a kind of a super school teaching a mass of different subjects, to which selected students are sent from other Shanghai schools for a period, not only to improve themselves, but to go back to their own schools and pass on the lessons they have learnt to others. We went to a musical performance played by a combination of pi pa, a stringed instrument, and concertinas, which was very gay. In the grounds there is a statue of Liu Hu Lan, a female

Boy playing concertina in the Children's Palace, Shanghai

Minhang, Shanghai's satellite town

martyr of the revolution killed in Shanxi province.

The Number One store employing 2,600 girls is on several floors and carries an immense range of goods, some at a price one would hardly have expected in such an egalitarian society. It is unpopular with the employees, who appear to be directed there and have small hopes of being transferred anywhere else. Opening hours are from 8 am to 8 pm.

A primary school, previously with 300 students and nine teachers had grown to one of 1,200 and 52 teachers; it had the usual wide range of subjects and for sport played ping pong and basket ball and also went in for long distance running. Peasants, soldiers and workers were encouraged to visit the school and give talks on their various employments, while the children also went out to the countryside to see the peasants working. At question time I asked the head boy what he wanted to do in later life; he said he wanted to be a worker in a commune. A girl, asked the same question, said her personal choice was to become a doctor, but hastily qualified this by saying that this would of course be dependent on a decision by the state. Students are not encouraged to have glamorous ideas about their future occupations. I noticed that from time to time all the pupils stopped work for five minutes and did eye exercises.

I had been told in Peking that the two British banks with headquarters in Hongkong, the Chartered and the Hongkong and Shanghai, had branches in Shanghai and decided to pay them a visit. Shades of bygone glory—their two offices were next door to each other in a rather dingy back street with some fifteen Chinese employees in each; I found Mr. Meiklejohn, manager of the Hongkong and Shanghai Bank, in his office and said I had called in case he wanted any letters taking home, as I was leaving the next day. "How do you find life in Shanghai?" I asked. "It's hell" he replied quite simply. "Apart from visiting the International Club, where all the notices are in Chinese, which I don't understand, there is little to interest one outside one's work, though I do have a car, which is the first owned by anyone in the bank here. My wife sits in our small flat and knits and sews. There is no sporting recreation like golf".

"How many people are there in the city with British passports?" I asked.

"Exactly seven" he replied "of which three are in the two banks and the remaining four at the Fu Dan university". Before the revolution there had probably been 20,000 British people living in this great city.

It was very interesting to visit the publishers of a Shanghai newspaper, the *Wen Hui Bao*, which had a circulation of about 900,000, all sent by post to regular subscribers. It had had a fairly chequered career as one might expect. Founded in 1937 as a bourgeois democratic paper, it had since 1949 represented the broad masses of the people. In the early days of the Cultural Revolution in 1967 it had been taken over by rightists favouring Liu Shao Qhi, but pressure by the staff changed the policy in favour of Chairman Mao shortly after. It had been under the influence of Jiang Qing from 1972 to 1974, but of course condemned the Gang of Four at the appropriate time in 1976.

Five hundred people were employed, split about evenly between the logistics, editorial and printing departments. Articles appeared to be the work of groups and not individual journalists. It encouraged correspondence with the public and printed articles about citizens who had helped the community, such as bus drivers with a particularly good record of helping passengers, a weaver with a particularly good production record and a boy who had found a hand bag containing money and several watches which he had turned in to a public security office. They had run a campaign criticising the Shanghai bus service and invited people to send in complaints about it. Prominence had been given to the fifth volume of Mao's works. Government policies and edicts were of course published in full.

I had already seen the difficult printing problems arising from the nature of the language at a book printing establishment in Peking; these are aggravated with a newspaper where speed is more important though the type still has to be set by hand. This paper was based on the use of between 4,000 and 5,000 of the most common characters. It had only four pages—the addition of another one or two would have created space problems owing to the need to have a bigger reserve of characters for type setting. The printing machines came from East Germany —a good machine, though very noisy.

No advertising is allowed in Chinese newspapers, so that revenue must derive entirely from subscriptions. Any significant increase in circulation would pose printing problems already described. Murders, sex, pornography and such like are rigidly excluded. Politically the editor must follow the party line in all things. It was a very slow moving process compared to the hectic rush in a newspaper office in the West.

And so back on an Air France plane to Paris via Peking and Karachi. And thereby hangs the tale of the party we had believed to have something to do with education, for it too was on the plane, which made a stop of some two hours in Peking, where the passengers were allowed into the very spacious waiting hall. The man we had referred to as a typical public schoolmaster was standing in the middle of the hall, hands behind his back, talking non-stop to another member of the party and my son said, "I'll bet you anything, dad, that man will at any minute move up and down on his toes—all schoolmasters do it" —and within 30 seconds he duly did just that, thus finally convincing us that our judgement had been right.

The party whose occupation we had so firmly established was installed in the VIP section in the forward compartment of the plane and I simply had to get confirmation that our theory was right, so I moved forward into their compartment, saw an empty seat next to a man reading a book and sat down in it, at the same time excusing myself for the intrusion. "My son and I" I said "have come to the conclusion that your party is in some way concerned with British education, and I simply wanted to confirm it".

"You are quite right" he replied, "I am the Vice-Chancellor of Durham University, the man behind me the Vice-Chancellor of Oxford and the other man over there the Regius Professor of Chemistry at Cambridge". We had stumbled on what was probably the most prestigious British educational delegation ever to have visited China.

XI
Tourism on the Grand Scale

High-rise Hongkong

THE "Lure of the East" is no empty phrase. Many of us with experience of it return there again and again. Is it curiosity? Or the complete contrast with life in the West? Or is it amazement that nearly a billion people, more than a fifth of the total population of our world, can be fed and clothed with no apparent signs of hunger, beggary or destitution? Have we not got something to learn from this society which orders its affairs and its human relations so well?

It was just over three years since my last visit when I came back in December 1980 for the third time since the Revolution— a very different visit from the two previous ones which had involved much travel and many visits to schools, hospitals, factories and communes in the company of an interpreter from the China International Travel Service, each visit lasting three weeks during the summer months. This one only lasted for a week and mainly concerned a gathering of tour operators and travel agents from the UK, the USA and Europe who had been

Sun Yat Sen Memorial Hall, Canton

invited by the CITS to discuss future plans for tourism. In-
vitations were sent out to 300 individuals—a further 1,200
applied, an indication of the great interest being taken in China.
Most of the UK contingent came by air to Hongkong, a journey
of about 16 hours, including one stop of about an hour at Dubai
on the Persian Gulf. Thence, after a night in a Hongkong hotel,
by air to Canton, which takes about 25 minutes. We had
originally been scheduled to go from Hongkong to Canton by
train, but this had for some reason been cancelled. Last minute
alterations to travel schedules are pretty common due, I suspect,
to shortage of transport facilities for the numbers travelling. On
the return journey we were due to go from Canton back to
Hongkong by hovercraft, but this too was cancelled and we
went back by air.

We spent the best part of a day in Canton. A bus tour of the
city with lunch at the Garden restaurant and a brief stop at the
memorial to Sun Yat Sen, the doyen of China's revolutionaries,
had been arranged. It consists of a large Memorial Hall, a
statue of the revolutionary himself and an ornate entrance arch,
all carried out in traditional Chinese style. Canton, the capital
of Guangdong province with a population of five million, was
for many years the centre of revolutionary activity against the
emperors of the Qing dynasty and more recently of Communist
supporters against Chiang Kai Shek, many of whom were
executed during a rising in 1927. A memorial park commem-

Peking's new international airport

orates the martyrs of this uprising, but we had no time to visit it.

The city has quite a mild climate in winter and trees somewhat like bougainvilleas were in flower on the streets. At another point in a public park a flower show was in full swing, with big arrangements of what looked chrysanthemums. Flowers are part and parcel of Chinese life, both in the world of art and floral decoration. Superb displays of azaleas and other flowering shrubs are not uncommon at railway stations.

The Cantonese dialect, said to contain nine tones instead of the four in Mandarin, unintelligible to northern Chinese and certainly to me, must be a holy terror to language students and I was surprised to find myself talking quite freely in Mandarin with members of the younger generation. I had always understood that Mandarin was to become the spoken language of the entire nation and here was proof of it.

Back in the airport lounge a loudspeaker was playing a cheerful Strauss waltz and there was a general air of relaxation and bonhomie, with no sign of the segregation of Chinese from foreigners, which had been so noticeable in 1974 and 1977.

The plane which took us to Peking was the same Trident we had been in from Hongkong, the journey taking about two-and-a-half hours. It was a complete surprise to land at Peking's new international airport, only opened in January 1980, capable of handling 1,500 passengers an hour and at the time of our arrival almost completely deserted. There is a bi-weekly service of Boeing 747s to Gatwick shared alternately by British Airways and the China Airline; a great expansion of foreign traffic is obviously expected. The original airport must still be serving the internal services.

We were housed in the Yuyi Bing Guan or Friendship Hotel, a collection of four large, modern and rather austere buildings which had been erected in the 1950s to house 2,000 Russian technicians, and is now the home of many long-stay foreigners such as teachers of English, students, business men and specialists of all kinds. A large communal dining room, far removed from the bedrooms, provides the meals, which were Chinese style food and eaten with chopsticks. Conversation at the circular tables to seat eight persons, as is the Chinese custom, was like the tower of Babel, with English predominating and it being used for conference purposes. It is incidentally the first foreign language in nearly all the schools, having displaced Russian in the 1960s. I had a single bedroom all to myself, well heated and with bathroom attached. The one great disadvantage of the Friendship Hotel is its distance from the centre of the city; there are certainly bus services but one needs to be young and active to use them.

The proceedings of the conference, which lasted for two days, took place in a spacious modern theatre-cum-lecture hall inside the Great Hall of the People made available by the Government —a signal honour, as the Great Hall, where meetings of the Peoples' National Congress and other august bodies take place, is a kind of Holy of Holies in the new Republic. It was built, along with nine other major public buildings in Peking, in 10 months in 1958/59, in order to be ready for the celebration of the tenth anniversary of the proclamation of the People's Republic on October 1, 1959. The year 1958 was the year of the "Great Leap Forward", when the entire working population was called on to work long hours almost beyond the limits of human endurance. As one young Chinese explained to me, massive projects of this kind are made possible by the "strategy of marshalling the human sea", for which there are plenty of precedents in history, such as the building of the Grand Canal to link the Yangtse and Yellow rivers in the Sixth Century AD and the completion of the Great Wall in the Qin dynasty (221 to 210 BC).

The Great Hall itself, facing on to the Tien An Men square is of imposing proportions and contains all that is best in the art and craftsmanship of the country. Provision is made for national occasions in the superb theatre accommodating 5,000 people and the dining hall, which can also seat 5,000 or take up to 10,000 for

The Great Hall of the People, Peking

a buffet meal. The dark red drapes shutting off the stage from the auditorium in the theatre carry a large circular golden plaque featuring the Wu Xing Qi or Five Star Flag, China's national emblem; red leather seats, each provided with a head phone, match the red of the drapes, while at a central point in the roof of the auditorium is a circular roof light illuminated by a myriad small electric bulbs, with the five star emblem in the middle,

The Dining Hall set for a banquet

The Theatre

the whole designed to convey the impression of a sunflower.

The provinces have not been overlooked, for each one of them, with the significant inclusion of Taiwan, and the major cities of Peking, Shanghai and Tientsin, has its own reception room furnished and decorated with all that is best in its own individual products and artwork. Ornate screens and large pictures in the traditional style of Chinese painting dominate most of the rooms; floors are either of polished wood or covered with carpets of the deepest pile, a traditional industry in some parts of the country. At some points huge ceramic urns in gay colours are placed on floors and I remember particularly one vase taller than almost any human being. Lesser vessels contain shrubs or bonsai trees. Smaller objets d'art tend to be lost owing to the sheer size of the rooms.

Not being either a tour operator or a travel agent myself I will not spend too much time discussing details of the business sessions. When I first came back to China in 1974, there were virtually no tourists at all; China had been almost a closed book to foreigners from the West ever since October 1949, except for a few business men who got visas and an occasional industrial exhibition from abroad. By 1977 tourism had begun to increase and there were 10,000 in that year, a number which had grown to 200,000 by 1980, this number being exclusive of the numerous overseas Chinese, who are administered by a different government department and many of whom have relatives on the mainland. Family ties are strong and many, particularly in the southern provinces of Guangdong and Fujian, receive remittances from well-to-do relations abroad, this providing a valuable source of foreign currency to the Government.

The head of the CITS estimated that it could deal with 800,000 foreign tourists by 1985, provided the current hotel building programme kept pace. Lack of hotels and poor communications have hitherto been the main obstacles to progress. A new "Great Wall Hotel" with 1,000 beds and American participation was to be built near Peking. The Chinese have much to learn about the habits and customs of foreigners, one in particular being the different hours to which most of them are accustomed. Programmes tend to start quite early in the morning and finish early in the afternoon; there is practically no night life in the cities, where everything closes down by about 10 pm. Control and administration of the large numbers expected will be important; I have already mentioned the tendency to make last minute changes in the routing of passengers; in October a large contingent of tourists due to be put up in Peking had to be sent to a seaside resort miles away at the last minute. There are at the moment only four major hotels in the capital.

Top table laid for travel agents' banquet

With the intention of showing the operators and agents something of the countryside round Peking, of letting them sample the train service and of showing them a minor tourist attraction which had only just been opened to foreigners, the CITS had arranged for a contingent to visit a place called Chengde about 130 miles northeast of Peking; the best part of two days was allotted for the visit. The train was due to leave Peking's main station at 6.30 am and the bus taking the contingent arrived with only minutes to spare. Departures and arrivals of trains, which travel at rather low speeds, are extremely punctual and we had literally to run through the milling crowds to catch it. The density of a Chinese crowd at a main line railway terminus has to be experienced to be believed, and there is always the thought at the back of one's mind that one is going to be swallowed up in it and never seen again. The train journey was uneventful, the only excitement being provided by the sight of a rather broken down, hardly recognisable section of the Great Wall snaking up and down a mountain side, which everyone tried to photograph.

Arrived at Chengde we walked through a milling crowd down to two or three small waiting buses which took us the short distance to the recently built forty roomed tourist hotel. The

Fu Ning Si temple at Chengde

crowd showed great interest in us and our belongings, which indicated that not many foreigners had previously visited the place.

Chengde is quite a small industrial town with a coal industry which produced a lot of coal dust. All 40 rooms in the hotel are twin-bedded—doubling up in the hotels is widespread in order to accommodate more people. The main attraction, indeed the sole attraction, as far as I could judge, is the Summer Palace built in the 18th Century for the Qing dynasty emperors as a summer resort away from Peking, and three temples built in the reign of Qian Long (1736–1795). In the afternoon we walked through the corridors, halls and rooms of the Palace and saw the room, with its yellow cushioned throne, where Lord Macartney and his ill fated mission had been received by Qian Long in 1793. At several points there were displays of handicrafts, scrolls, postcards and other items, all at fixed prices, anything over a hundred years old being provided with a red seal. Outside in the gardens and pleasure ground everything was frozen hard and it was a relief to get back to the well heated hotel. Here the plumbing was playing tricks, water sometimes being unobtainable and at others cascading out of the taps, where people had inadvertently forgotten to turn them off. I was woken up at 2 a.m. by the sound of a mighty rushing stream to find a steam filled bathroom and a cascade of steaming hot water from the hot tap in the sink.

The next morning we set off in the direction of the three temples just outside the town. The first, called the Fu Ning Si, which had a small factory right opposite its entrance, had been built by Qian Long in honour of a prince who had put down a serious rising in the far off province of Xinjiang. The main hall of the temple contained what was said to be the biggest Buddha in the world, and surrounding him many smaller Lohans; it was so cold (the temperature that morning was -19 degrees Centigraded) that I failed to take in much of what the guide was saying. I do remember that the giant Buddha and his satellites were covered with a good deal of dust. The two other temples were both built to celebrate Qian Long's 70th birthday, when both the Panchen Lama from Lhasa and the Dalai Lama from Mongolia paid a state visit to the Palace; one of them bears a striking resemblance to the Potala Palace in Lhasa.

I was not impressed with the visits to the Summer Palace and its temples. There was no sign of any recent paint work and dust was everywhere. The equivalent of our Department of the Environment must have immense tasks to deal with in Peking and had probably not been able to do much here. Chengde should never be visited in the depths of winter—it was sheer purgatory.

Before we went out on the morning of the second day I had arranged a time call to my daughter in Scotland at 7 am my time and 11 pm hers. The reception was perfect and I could hear every word distinctly—far more clearly in fact than in many a local call at home. We spoke for four minutes, the total cost of which was 38 Chinese yuan or about £10 sterling. Quite a gathering of elderly Chinese were listening to the call, which I suddenly realised had cost the equivalent of about one month's wages for a poorly-paid job in China. Did they think I was a millionaire or just clean crazy? They made no comment either to me or each other, their faces remaining devoid of any sign of interest, of surprise or of any other human emotion. This is of course what gives rise to the reputation of the Chinese for being inscrutable.

Chinese television had been taking an interest in our proceedings and members of their crew were in the saloon coach of our train on the way back to Peking, as well as a Chinese army officer, distinguished by having four pockets on his tunic, as opposed to the two worn by other ranks, but no badge of rank. He was adjudged by one of the Chinese to be of rather senior rank owing to the size of his stomach! Just as in the airport lounge at Canton the atmosphere in our coach on the train was relaxed and congenial with no sign of any segregation of our Chinese friends—a welcome change from three years previously.

On the day after our arrival I found time to spend one full day on a commune just outside Peking, which I had previously arranged with the authorities; I had been there once before, but only briefly. The communes, initially regarded as agricultural producers after their formation in 1958, have since, with government encouragement and financial help, diversified considerably. This one, for instance, has 12 production units of various sizes, three of which I visited, one making heating boilers, another turning out screws and a third small plastic components for radio sets, these being sub-contracted by a firm completing the sets in the city. Nearly 20 per cent of the able bodied workers in the commune were working in the production plants, which adds variety to the jobs available and tends to be more profitable than those in agriculture.

As an example of the government's active promotion of development and diversification in the communes there was a huge new greenhouse covering nearly two hectares, for the construction of which the government had made an outright grant of four million yuan (about £1 million) to which the commune had added a further one million yuan from its accumulation fund. The greenhouse, roofed with Japanese fibre glass, was mass producing cucumbers and tomatoes for the Peking market.

This commune, like any other, is an integrated social unit as well as being an agricultural producer and manufacturer. Administered by an elected committee with an elected chairman responsible to the central government, it provides services like schools, hospitals, kindergartens and the village shop, all of which I went to. In this community of 43,000 people there had been 710 live births in 1980, giving a birth rate of about 1.7 per cent, which must be slightly above the national average, as one might expect in a rural community.

Peking has grown considerably since 1977, its continually rising population now growing up towards the nine million mark, as evidenced by the great growth in the number of blocks of flats and the fearful overcrowding on public transport. Building up the infrastructure, while providing employment, diverts capital from the Four Modernisations programme and underlines the importance of population control, which is obviously realised by the government now seeking to limit families to one child and imposing significant penalties in the housing field for families exceeding that number. The previous scheme called for the limitation of families to two children. The number of the small Tientsin jeeps serving the armed forces

Mass production of tomatoes and cucumbers

seemed to have increased but there was no significant increase in the traffic on the roads nor had there been any visible change in the system of traffic control.

Some years ago publicity was being given to Peking's underground railway, which then disappeared from the headlines. I concluded that it must have been incorporated in the honeycomb of air raid shelters under the city, which the Chinese are proud to show to visitors and indeed showed to a number of ours. I discovered that it was in fact running over a limited stretch and determined to try it out. Hiring a taxi, I jumped off at the An Ding Men station and told the driver to go to the next stop and wait for me there, then descended the stairs to the platform, which could not have been more than 15 metres below ground at most. The large crowd surged forward as the train came in, and I was squirted into it rather like tooth paste from a tube. The little train which had rattled in seemed very small and toylike; high frequency of trains will be needed if much impact is to be made on the population's travel problems by this little railway.

Not far from the centre of Peking and the central east-west axis, the Chang An Jie, or street of everlasting peace, lies the Roman Catholic Nan Tang or South Cathedral which I visited. It is remarkable that Christianity should have survived so many vicissitudes in this Marxist atheistic country and that this church not only had a congregation of 6,000 but intended Christmas services in two churches in the city. I also visited a much smaller Protestant church which had a following of 600 and had a font for baptisms in the way that I am accustomed to and a kind of cistern below some floor boards containing water for the complete immersion of the person to be baptised in; I had never realised that members of the Baptist church were baptised this manner. Both priest and pastor told me that quite a high proportion of their adherents were young people.

All Christian churches were closed for the duration of the Cultural Revolution, priests and pastors being sent down to the communes to work in the fields. It is not long since they have been re-opened for worship.

Mao's mausoleum on the Tian An Men square, still under construction in 1977, is now complete and open to the public; its rather squat proportions seem wrong to me and architecturally not up to the standards of other post-revolutionary buildings in the square. Large crowds were waiting in long queues to enter the hall and file past the "Great Helmsman" as he was often called. For some reason the hall is only open on three days of the week. I joined the silent queue with my Chinese companion and filed past the embalmed body resting on a plinth inside a glass case and raised some two and a half feet above floor level. Four or five soldiers armed with pistols were unobtrusively strolling about inside the hall, which reminded me of the two soldiers with rifles and fixed bayonets guarding the entrance to Lenin's tomb on the Red Square in Moscow, which they freely make use of if any of the waiting crowds fall out of line.

Nearby in the Ministry of Justice Jiang Qing, Mao's widow, was on trial for her life on charges of plotting against the state and committing atrocities and excesses during the Cultural Revolution. The disclosures which have come to light during the trial may have somewhat tarnished the image of Mao, but he is still regarded as the man who put China on its feet and on the map. Nothing will erase the memories of the historic Long March in 1934/35, of Mao's resistance to the Japanese invaders and his crushing victory against Chiang K'ai Shek against overwhelming material odds.

The arrest of the Gang of Four shortly after Mao's death in 1976, hailed with relief by most of the Chinese people, removed the shackles on art, literature and the theatre rigidly imposed by Jiang Qing. Controls were repressive in the extreme; only themes with the purest revolutionary content passed the censor. All this has changed with a return to more traditional themes and a more liberal attitude to foreign art and literature. Foreign music is frequently broadcast in public places; even a disco has been started for the benefit of foreign visitors. Shakespeare's plays are in vogue and, as in Russia, the works of Robert Burns are highly regarded and being translated into Chinese; a Burns Supper with Scottish participation cannot be far away.

The finding and unearthing near Xian of the great underground army guarding the tomb of the Emperor Qin, who died in 210 BC, has been given wide publicity in the world's press and media. Specimens of two of the men and a horse were on view in one of the buildings in the Imperial Palace, each absolutely perfect and without blemish after a life below ground of nearly 2,200 years. These were no mass-produced men; each had a distinct personality of his own. They are a light grey in colour, short in stature and wearing a kind of bonnet and knicker-bockers. Dust off the Gobi desert has helped to preserve the many buried treasures in this part of China. Many more will come to light, indeed are coming to light, as China develops and the earth's crust is disturbed.

As readers will remember from previous chapters there is always a "Theme of the Moment" in China; in 1974 it was the Lin Biao/Confucius syndrome; in 1977 the "Gang of Four" and

Jiang Qing on trial at the Ministry of Justice

Poster advertising in the new consumer society

in 1980 more generally the "Four Modernisations" (of industry, agriculture, science and technology and the armed forces). The largely political themes have been succeeded by the economic, as one would expect from a regime dominated by Deng Xiao Ping, the arch pragmatist once labelled as a "Capitalist Roader" and nearly expelled from the Communist Party. Politics were no longer in command to the same extent, and the experts were taking precedence over the Reds. The emphasis was on economic revival and progress.

When introducing a new initiative on a grand scale the Chinese, in a wave of euphoria and optimism, often overstate the case and predict the unattainable. Mao's initiative of the "Great Leap Forward" in 1958, which foundered in a sea of unrealistic estimates and false statistics, was a glaring case of this. From many conversations with Chinese young and old I formed the impression that the "Four Modernisations" introduced with a tremendous fanfare in 1977 were not achieving the results expected or fulfilling the targets laid down. No specific reasons were given for this, beyond general statements about the difficulty of eradicating "feudalism" and fear of the growing power and dead hand of the bureaucracy. By "feudalism" is meant a return to old pre-revolutionary habits and practices, such as nepotism, self-aggrandisement, dislike of soiling one's hands by manual work and lack of contact with the people. Mao foresaw the dangers of a growing bureaucracy remote from the daily lives and work of the people, when he ordered his Red Guards during the Cultural Revolution to "bombard the headquarters", meaning to attack the cadres of the Communist Party and those in positions of responsibility.

China is numerically still a nation of peasants. Liberation was peasant-based; Mao understood them and the commune system has worked pretty well. Not so industry, which has been totally centralised, with wages, hours of work and conditions of employment laid down by the government for the whole country. Trade unions are an organ of the government and have no say in those matters for which they exist in the West. Steps are now being taken to decentralise authority and give more scope to managers on the spot. The first foreign country to be visited by Mao's appointed successor Hua Guo Feng was Yugoslavia, which has decentralised in just this way. In some cases profits earned by an enterprise, instead of being handed over to the central government, are being ploughed back into the enterprise for further development. An indication of the widening of differentials in the pay structure is the imposition for the first time of an income tax on the higher salary grades. This would have been anathema to Mao's communist idealism, where the emphasis was on narrowing differentials, money being an irrelevance, workers not being there to better themselves but to "serve the people".

The country suffers from a chronic shortage of foreign exchange, as a partial remedy for which industries are being set up with capital jointly owned by the government and the foreign company concerned. In some cases repayment of capital or the service of interest charges have been offered in kind rather than cash.

The busy week was nearly over. December is not the ideal month in which to visit Peking and North China; the choice of month was dictated by the fact that it is a slack time for the tourist industry in the West before the pressure is on in January, the busiest month for bookings. Snow and ice regrettably made it impossible for all but a few who got there by train to visit the Great Wall, in spite of many efforts to reach it by bus and taxi. What a calamity; fancy consulting a travel agent who had spent a week in and around Peking and hadn't even seen one of the Seven Wonders of the World.

Back to Canton it was a Boeing 707. Space in the plane was very cramped—extra seats might have been added to increase the payload. More gifts and souvenirs were handed out—a car keyring, two pokes of sweets, an address book and a book of paper cut-outs. There was some time to spare and we again had a meal in the Garden Restaurant. Back at the airport there was some delay and confusion. The Chinese yuan or dollar has no value outside the country and had to be changed into other currencies, a lengthy proceeding. There was a customs and passport check. One disadvantage of group travel is that passports are taken away by the organisers who give details to the Chinese embassy concerned, which approves the names of the group as a whole and does not stamp each individual passport with a visa; a visa covering a trip to China in the early days of tourism can be greatly prized and many requests were being made for the passport checkers to stamp passports with a Chinese character, admittedly a poor substitute for a visa. Finally it was the boarding cards which had not been issued to individuals.

Hongkong with its skyscrapers, busy streets and fast moving traffic is a complete contrast to any of the cities in mainland China, though some of the older, narrower streets hung with gay banners and colourful neon lights are very reminiscent of streets on the mainland before the Revolution. It is a bargain basement for many things, particularly in the electronic and new technology fields. Hardly had we set foot in it before the two journalists in our party were off to buy the latest in tape recorders far cheaper than in the UK. Somewhere there is a replica of a village as seen during the Song dynasty (979–1126 AD), but unfortunately I had no time to visit it.

The whole journey back to Gatwick took place in complete darkness; we left at 8.30 pm and reached Gatwick at 5.30 am the next morning, half an hour ahead of schedule. The stop at Dubai enabled one to get a breath of fresh air and stretch one's legs; there is a big duty free wine store there with a wide variety of spirits and I bought a bottle of VSOP brandy. It had been an exhausting trip for a septuagenarian, but rewarding none the less. China, so long asleep and oblivious of the world outside it, has woken up and is a force to be reckoned with; the more the foreign visitors go there, the better.

Epilogue

THE decision to open up China to a large scale invasion of foreign visitors is a very recent one; three years in the life of a nation with a civilisation going back to about 2,500 BC and a history of virtual seclusion from most of the rest of the world for the whole of that period, is but a moment in time. Small wonder that the Chinese find the antics of some of the visitors surprising and equally that some of the latter are surprised by what they see. The language is a barrier to understanding and even the fact that English is generally regarded by them as the first foreign language will not entirely fill the gap. There has got to be a mutual understanding of each other's language and the growth in the number of students learning Chinese in the UK is encouraging.

If you happen to be one of those considering a visit to China for the first time, I can assure you that you will find a warm welcome and friendship there. Tourism to them of course is an important way of relieving foreigners of some of their cash, but this is done in quite an unobtrusive and charming way; they want their visitors to take away the best possible impressions of what they have seen. The CITS interpreters and guides are thoughtful and considerate, but remember that, if you make a request to see some special place or activity which they cannot meet, they will not turn it down flat, but sidetrack the issue and say that it is not convenient or that the place is too far away. The words "Yes" and "No" do not exist in their language. Protocol and good manners demand a reply which may be thought evasive, but the evasion should be immediately apparent and the subject dropped.

In their eyes tourists are "playing themselves". The Chinese from the mainland you meet travelling abroad are all doing a job of work. "Holidays with pay" are quite unknown in China and it will be many years before they will be able to afford the luxury of foreign tours. By our standards their standard of living is very low, though their cost of food is much lower than ours. The average citizen, if a town dweller, almost certainly lives in a house belonging to the Government; his possessions are few, not extending far beyond the clothes he stands up in, a watch, bicycle, radio, possibly a camera and if he is particularly well off a TV. If he rides in a car, it will not be his, but a taxi or a vehicle belonging to a business or a state official. If you travel in a plane with a contingent of Chinese on board, you will probably find that they will have nearly left the tarmac, before the baggage-laden tourists start debouching from the plane. They live sparingly, keep fit on it and have the bare minimum of personal belongings.

The most dangerous, almost irresponsible, thing any writer can do is to make prophecies about the future, particularly in the case of China, which was once described to me as a "one off" country, which often took the most unexpected initiatives. Who else but they would have thought of introducing a new era of understanding with the USA by organising a ping pong match?

I believe that much of the long term success of the "Four Modernisations" programme will depend on the outcome of efforts to control the growth of the population. Failure to keep up the momentum of material progress will lead to disagreements at the top, which are always dangerous.

In a country where a very few rule the destinies of a great many and where there has been a long tradition of all powerful Emperors, it is probably an advantage to have an outstanding figure at the top. The death of Mao can be equated with the death of Stalin, both dictators and despots. It took some time before Khrushchev emerged as Stalin's successor; perhaps Mao's is still in the making. Deng Xiao Bing, of whom much is heard is too old.

The Chinese have always been very sensitive about their borders, the threat to which comes from Vietnam in the south and Outer Mongolia in the north, both satellites of the USSR. For years the Chinese have been warning the rest of the world of the Russian desire and aim to dominate the world; on the face of it there is little likelihood of a reconciliation between the two. Should it come to a war, Manchuria, vital to the economy, is dangerously isolated and could be cut off from mainland China without much difficulty.

People who view with alarm the fact that China is Communist can have little idea of the chaotic state of the country in the early 1930s, made much worse by 17 years of constant war and civil strife. If ever a country needed a strong hand it was China, and Mao provided it; democracy in our sense of the word had been tried for decades and found wanting. Today Communist Party rule is total and reaches right down to the grass roots of society, but there are many indications of the return of capitalist enterprise; one of the first things they will tell you when you visit a commune is the total amount of savings held by their members in the bank. The Chinese are a pragmatic people who know on which side their bread is buttered; the Russians would have taken over Hongkong years ago.

And so I wish the Chinese people well and hope they will enjoy a further long period of peace in which to modernise their country. "Yi lu ping an" as they say when you set out on a journey "One road level and peaceful."